TV DINNERS
AND OTHER MEDIA MUNCHIES

Dear Chris,
Happy 32nd and many more!
Love,
Veronica, Dennie & Ryan

FAVORITE RECIPES FROM THE WASHINGTON BROADCAST COMMUNITY

TV DINNERS
AND OTHER MEDIA MUNCHIES

by The Washington Chapter,
The National Academy of Television Arts and Sciences

ACROPOLIS BOOKS LTD.
WASHINGTON, D.C.

National Academy of Television Arts and Sciences "TV Dinners" Committee
Frances Stachow Seeger, Chairman
Jeanne Bowers
Pam Simon
Sue Ann Staake

Cover Design and Divider Pages: Hank & Anne Zangara

Photography: Ron Fine

Copyright 1986 by The Washington Chapter, The National Academy of Television Arts and Sciences. All rights reserved.
Except for inclusion of brief quotations in a review, no part of this book may be reproduced or utilized in any form or by any means, electronic or mechanical, including photo-copying, recording or by any information storage and retrieval system, without permission in writing from the publisher.

ACROPOLIS BOOKS, LTD.
Colortone Building,
2400 17th St., N.W., Washington, D.C. 20009

Book Design: Pamela Moore
Art Director: Robert Hickey

Printed in the United States of America by
COLORTONE PRESS, Creative Graphics, Inc.,
Washington, D.C. 20009

Attention: Schools and Corporations
ACROPOLIS books are available at quantity discounts with bulk purchase for educational, business, or sales promotional use. For information, please write to: SPECIAL SALES DEPARTMENT, ACROPOLIS BOOKS LTD., 2400 17th ST., N.W., WASHINGTON, D.C. 20009

Are there Acropolis Books you want
but cannot find in your local store?
You can get any Acropolis book title in print. Simply send title and retail price, plus 50 cents per copy to cover mailing and handling costs for each book desired. District of Columbia residents add applicable sales tax. Enclose check or money order only, no cash please, to:
ACROPOLIS BOOKS LTD.,
2400 17th St., N.W., WASHINGTON, D.C. 20009

Library of Congress Cataloging in Publication Data

Washington Chapter, The National Academy of Television Arts and Sciences,
T.V. dinners, and other media munchies
1. Cooking, Recipes   2. Seeger, Frances Stachow, editor
ISBN 0-87491-816-2

Table of Contents

Introduction   6

Appetizers, Soups and Salads   10
Great starts to any meal, ranging from simple to elegant . . . an appetizer, soup or salad to suit every taste.

Maincourses   46
Maincourse choices for 24 hours a day . . . breakfast specials, simple sandwiches, 5 different chili recipes, one dish meals, beef, chicken, seafood, pork, and a smattering of international cuisine.

Vegetables and Side Dishes   136
A selection of vegetables, potatoes, pasta and rice for a nice addition to any meal.

Desserts   156
Pies, cakes, cookies, candy and other favorites to satisfy every sweet tooth in town.

The Leftovers   198
Beverages, breads, bachelor fare, trash and flash dining, an anchorwoman's dinner, measurements, and much much more.

About N.A.T.A.S.   219

About BCDC   220

Index   221

Introduction

When the Washington Chapter of the National Academy of Television Arts and Sciences decided to publish a cookbook, no one quite knew what to expect. We knew our fellow broadcasters loved to eat and that they could usually be counted on to bring interesting or imaginative dishes to parties. But we were not sure what reflections of culinary expertise we'd find. What emerged from the Washington broadcast community and parents at the Broadcasters' Child Development Center is an interesting collection . . . from bachelor fare to international cuisine, and a lot of just "plain good eating" recipes. To a large extent, the recipes reflect the hectic pace, and 24 hour-a-day routine of the business. You'll find a lot of easy to prepare recipes, some from scratch and some with the help of prepared foods. Generally, the recipes are the kind that you can actually make after a busy day at work and not the kind you just read and wish you had time to prepare. In each section, you will find those, however, that are more complex and require some extra effort . . . perhaps best suited for company or the weekend.

In Maincourses you'll note that chicken was the most popular ingredient with many one-dish meals included. And don't be surprised with the number of breakfast and sandwich selections. In the TV and radio business . . . those meals are often the main meal of the day. In The Leftovers, you'll be treated to John Goldsmith's advice on eating right from the vending machine, tips from bachelors on how they survive, and to Susan King's guide to preparing a dinner for guests between the 6 o'clock news and the 11 o'clock news.

Many who submitted recipes, use cooking as a time to relax and be creative, so we were often confronted with converting "a glob of this," "as much as you like," or "whatever feels good" into cups and ounces. We tried to figure out what many contributors meant by "a large can," a "small can," or just a plain "can." Hopefully, we didn't miss any! While we didn't test every recipe, they were all reviewed by committee members who enjoy and understand cooking. We hope you'll enjoy our collection of favorites.

This book is being published as a fundraising project for the Broadcasters' Child Development Center which N.A.T.A.S. helped start six years ago. All of us associated with N.A.T.A.S. and BCDC have come to appreciate the value of top notch care the center provides and the importance of its availability to our children. While the center is self-sustaining, it, like all childcare centers, is in constant need of support to assure continued growth.

The project emerged over several years and contains recipes from both broadcast employees and parents at BCDC. We found in preparing the book that people frequently move from place to place rather quickly in TV and radio and the stations themselves change owners and even call letters. We did our best to reflect the current employers and call-letters, but there is no guarantee that there won't be changes between the time this book goes to the printer and the time it is published.

"TV Dinners" is really a success because of all those who took the time to share their favorite recipes with us. We want to thank all of those who contributed for their interest and support. A special thanks goes to Stephanie Campbell, who, as President of the Washington Chapter of N.A.T.A.S., gave new life to the project before moving to Miami last Fall. Sandy Reedy deserves thanks for coming up with the idea three years ago. Jeanne Bowers, Sue Ann Staake, Pam Simon, Gena Fitzgerald and Kate Atkins get heartfelt thanks for working so hard to pull the long-dormant project together. Finally thanks to Hank Zangara for his cover design and creative assistance and to all those at Acropolis Books who believed in our project and helped us so patiently.

We hope you enjoy using "TV Dinners . . . and Other Media Munchies," again and again!

Frances Stachow Seeger
Chairman,
N.A.T.A.S. Cookbook Committee

APPETIZERS, SOUPS & SALADS

STEPHEN RABIN is President, Educational Film Center, Annandale VA. He is a former director of Public Programs and Media Programs for the National Endowment for the Humanities. He has been associated with public broadcasting since 1962.

Stephen Rabin
Antipasto Concertina*

- 1 head red leaf lettuce
- 1 6½-ounce can solid white tuna, in oil
- 16 paper-thin slices genoa salami
- 16 paper-thin slices round provolone cheese
- 1 12-ounce can pitted black olives
- 1 10-ounce jar green olives with pimentos
- 1 6-ounce jar marinated artichoke hearts
- 1 6-ounce jar marinated mushrooms
- 1 9-ounce jar Tuscan green peppers
- 1 4-ounce jar sliced sweet pimentos
- 1 3-ounce can anchovy filets
- 1 pint cherry tomatoes
- 1 ounce red wine vinegar (approximate)
- 3 ounces Italian olive oil (approximate)
- Italian seasonings or oregano
- Large round platter

The secret to this dish is in the dressing. Before you begin work on the platter, mix up an oil and vinegar base to your taste in a jar but no more than 3-4 ounces. Add dash of Italian seasoning or oregano. As you build the platter, add a splash of liquid to the dressing base from each of the ingredients except tuna. Right, do not add the liquid from the salami or cheese, either. When finished, seal jar and refrigerate until ready to serve.

Now, arrange largest lettuce leaves around the platter with the red ends at outer edge. Drain oil from tuna, place tuna in center. Roll salami and cheese and alternate around the tuna like bicycle spokes. Place cherry tomatoes around tuna. Now let your free spirit take over. Decorate the platter with some sense of abandon using the black and green olives, artichoke hearts, mushrooms, peppers and anchovies. Finally, sprinkle sliced pimento where the color is needed.

About 15 minutes before serving, spoon dressing over antipasto platter. Serve with fresh Italian bread.

Serves: 6 very hungry cameramen
         8 somewhat hungry editors, or
         22 producers

"This recipe was found in a glass flask floating in the water at Fell's Point. Attached to it was this plaintive message . . . "We have lived on this during our entire crossing with crazy Christopher. Thank you lord, we reached land."

*"The title comes from the recipes ability to expand or contract for any number of guests"

JOHNNY HOLLIDAY is best known as the voice of the University of Maryland Terrapins on WMAL radio. His morning and afternoon sports reports are heard on the ABC Information Network. Johnny has worked at WMAL since 1979 and in Washington for 16 years.

Johnny Holliday
Apples Canapes

- 4 medium or large apples
- 2 cups white table wine or sherry (approximate)
- 5 slices bacon
- 3 ounces cream cheese at room temperature
- 2 tablespoons heavy cream or evaporated milk

Pare apples. Cut out apple balls with melon ball cutter. Place balls in quart jar; cover with wine. Let stand 2 to three hours. Fry bacon slowly until brown

TV Dinners
11

and crisp; drain on paper towel and crumble. Mix softened cream cheese and cream to right consistency to coat apple balls easily. Drain apple balls, roll in paper towel and dry. Coat each ball with cream cheese mixture and place toothpick in each ball. Dip one end of apple ball in crumbled bacon.

Serves: 8-10

NOTE: You can substitute ½ to ¾ cup chopped nuts for bacon.

DIANA ELY-EPSTEIN has been soothing listeners' ears at WMAL since 1977. A native Washingtonian, her broadcast talents have earned her roles in commercials, films, TV series and narrations, both regionally and nationally.

Diana Ely-Epstein
Baked Brie

- 1 4-ounce package Pillsbury Crescent Rolls
- 1 4½-ounce package Gerard Brie
- 1 egg, beaten
- 4 ounces sliced almonds
- Pam or other spray to grease cookie sheet

Pre-heat oven to 325 degrees.

On waxed paper, arrange dough in one big square. You can tear it in half at the seam and rearrange. Cover with another piece of wax paper. Then go over it a few strokes with a rolling pin to get all the edges nice and together. You should have a nice square of dough when you are finished.

Place the whole brie in the center of the dough. Do not remove the outer layer of cheese. Pull dough up over cheese and make a nice little package taking care to press all the edges of the dough snuggly together. Brush the beaten egg all over the top of the dough. Place on cookie sheet that has been sprayed with Pam or other non-stick coating. Sprinkle with sliced almonds.

Bake for 12-15 minutes at 325 degrees or until top is golden brown.

Remove from oven and cool 10 minutes before serving.

Serve alone or with crackers.

Serves: 4

"Makes a simply gourmet-looking hors d'oeuvre. Enjoy."

SANDY PASTOOR is vice president and programming director at WTTG and a former president of the Washington Chapter of N.A.T.A.S. Before coming to Washington in 1981, she worked in the Cincinnati TV market.

Sandy Pastoor
Boursin Cheese

    8 ounces whipped unsalted butter
   16 ounces cream cheese
    1 clove garlic, crushed
   ½ teaspoon salt
   ¼ teaspoon ground pepper
    1 tablespoon parsley
    1 teaspoon dill
    1 teaspoon basil
    1 teaspoon marjoram
    1 teaspoon thyme

Mix all ingredients together in mixing bowl until well blended. Mold with hands into desired shape or ball. Make in advance to allow flavors to blend.

Serves: 8-10

GENA FITZGERALD is a producer for News 7's investigative unit. She has worked with WJLA since 1978. When she isn't digging up stories, she's doing volunteer work with the Alexandria Urban Archeology Program.

Gena Fitzgerald
Boursin Spread

- 4 ounces camembert or brie cheese
- 8 ounces cream cheese
- 8 ounces whipping cream, well chilled
- ⅓ cup fresh parsley, chopped
- 1½ teaspoon thyme
- 1 large clove garlic, minced
- 1 teaspoon fresh ground pepper

Remove rind from camembert or brie. Soften the cheese along with cream cheese for at least 30 minutes.

In a mixing bowl, beat the whipping cream until it forms soft peaks. In another bowl, beat the cheeses together until well mixed. Fold in chopped parsley, then thyme, then garlic. By hand, fold in whipped cream. Chill thoroughly. Garnish with black pepper. Garnish with additional parsley, if desired. Serve with fresh french bread, crackers or fresh vegetables.

Serves: 8-10

STEVE HAGEDORN is a promotion writer and producer for WDCA-TV.

Steve Hagedorn
Deviled Eggs

- 6 hard cooked eggs, peeled
- 2 tablespoons mayonnaise
- 1 teaspoon vinegar
- ½ teaspoon salt
- Dash pepper
- 1 teaspoon prepared mustard
- ¼ teaspoon paprika
- 2-3 dashes tabasco sauce

Halve eggs lengthwise. Remove and mash yolks. Set whites aside. Combine mashed yolks with remaining ingredients. Fill reserved whites with yolk mixture and chill. Dust with paprika before serving.

Yields: 12

LINDA FANG works at WRC in the Programming Department.

Linda Fang
Chinese Meatballs

- 1 pound ground pork
- 1 teaspoon fine ground fresh ginger
- 1 tablespoon cooking wine
- ½ teaspoon salt
- 2 tablespoons vegetable oil
- 1 teaspoon Accent (optional)
- 2 tablespoons soy sauce
- 2 tablespoons chopped spring onion
- 1 tablespoon sugar
- 1 tablespoon water
- 1 egg white

Mix one tablespoon of water with ground pork, stir until smooth. Add spring onion, fresh ginger, wine, soy sauce, sugar, salt and stir again. Add egg white and stir until everything is well-blended together.

Pre-heat frying pan, add two tablespoons of oil, heat until warm, reduce heat. Use a tablespoon to scoop out a spoonful of ground pork.

Make a meatball with the help of the spoon and your hand. Put the meatball into the hot oil. Continue to make meatballs and cook them until they are brown on one side. Turn and cook the other side. Take out the brown ones and put in new ones. When all the meatballs are cooked, put them back in the pan. Add water and some soy sauce, sugar and salt. Cook on low heat until the sauce thickens and is almost absorbed by the meatballs. Add some Accent if preferred.

Serves: 6

"Delicious"

Note: Chopped fresh spring onions and ground fresh ginger are not available in stores. You have to prepare them yourself.

DAVID NUELL is station manager at WRC where he has worked since 1971. He joined the station as a news producer and also served as its news director.

David Nuell
Dill Dip and Vegetables

- 1 pint sour cream
- 2 cups mayonnaise
- 2 tablespoons dill, crushed
- 1 tablespoon onion powder
- 1½ teaspoons chives, chopped
- 1 tablespoon Beaumonde Seasoning (Spice Island Brand)
- Fresh vegetables—see suggestions below

Mix together all ingredients except fresh vegetables and chill in refrigerator overnight to allow flavors to blend.

To serve: Cut tops off of large red, green, and yellow peppers, remove seeds, rinse and pat dry. Fill peppers with dip. Place in center of platter, surround with carrots, celery, Chinese pea pods, Belgian endive, broccoli, red, green and yellow peppers, cucumber slices or other seasonal summer vegetables that have been cleaned and cut in serving pieces.

Serves: 10-15

"The recipe is from cooking instructor and family friend Sandy Sabel. The serving suggestions are mine."

Hot Crab Dips ... Three Variations

SUSAN KNIGHT is a designer with WJLA.

Susan Knight
Hot Crab Dip

- 8 ounces cream cheese, softened
- ¼ teaspoon curry powder
- 1 7-ounce can crabmeat

Drain crabmeat and pick over to remove shells. Mix all ingredients together well. Spoon into a ceramic crock such as empty Wispride cheese crock, or use small ovenproof casserole dish. Cover with foil. Bake for 20-25 minutes at 350 degrees or until dip bubbles. Serve hot with crackers.

Serves: 6-8

WALT STARLING has been a familiar voice to radio listeners for years in Washington. He can currently be heard on WCLY. He is glad to share credit for this recipe with Sharon Starling.

Walt Starling
Hot Crab Spread

- 8 ounces cream cheese, softened
- 1 tablespoon onion, finely chopped
- 1 teaspoon prepared horseradish
- 1 tablespoon mayonnaise
- 1 tablespoon milk
- 1 7-ounce can crabmeat
- 4 ounces slivered almonds

Rinse and drain crabmeat and remove shells. Combine cream cheese, onion, horseradish, mayonnaise and milk and mix until smooth. Blend in crabmeat by hand. Bake in ovenproof dish for 15 minutes at 350 degrees. Remove from oven and top with almonds. Return to oven for 5 minutes more. Serve hot with crackers.

Serves: 6-8

MARY LALOS has worked in the Executive Offices of WJLA for 6½ years. Her hot crab dip has gotten such rave reviews that she keeps a folder full of copies of the recipe in her desk. Now she can tell her fans that they can find it in "TV DINNERS."

Mary Lalos
Hot Crab Dip

- 1 7-ounce can crabmeat
- 8 ounces cream cheese at room temperature
- ½ cup mayonnaise or Miracle Whip
- 2 green onions, diced
-    Dash of tabasco sauce
- 1 teaspoon worcestershire sauce (approximate)
-    Dash of pepper
- 2-4 ounces sliced almonds

Drain crabmeat and remove shells. Blend together crabmeat, cream cheese, mayonnaise, onions, tabasco, worcestershire sauce, and pepper. Spread in ovenproof dish and spread sliced almonds over the top. Bake for 20 minutes at 350 degrees. Serve hot with pumpernickel bread or crackers.

Serves: 6-8

Appetizers

ANN AIKEN is a graphic artist who currently does freelance work for WRC-TV. She previously worked for WTOP-TV.

Ann Aiken
Dragon's Breath

- 1 10-ounce package frozen chopped spinach
- 3 cloves garlic, crushed
- 1 small onion, finely chopped
- 1 pint sour cream
- 1 cup mayonnaise
- 1 package (.4 ounce dry mix) ranch-style dressing mix
- 2 loaves round pumpernickel bread, unsliced

Cook and drain spinach, squeezing out excess water with spoon. Mix sour cream together with mayonnaise and dressing mix. Add spinach, chopped onion and crushed garlic.

Make a bowl out of one loaf of bread by cutting around the edge with a grapefruit knife and carefully removing the middle. Be sure to leave ½ inch shell at bottom. Fill the "bread bowl" with dip. Rip 2 inch pieces of bread from section that was removed and from extra loaf. To serve, arrange bread pieces around "bowl" on large platter.

Serves: 8-10

BILL CERRI is another of those veteran voices of Washington radio. He's been sharing his talents with listeners of WETA-FM for years.

Bill Cerri
Horseradish Pie

- 4 cups fresh grated horseradish
- 2 cups parmesan cheese
- 1½ teaspoons baking powder
- 2 tablespoons vegetable oil
- Black pepper to taste
- 14 eggs

Mix ingredients thoroughly. Pour into 10 or 12" skillet coated with a little oil. Be sure you use a skillet with a handle that won't burn in the oven, such as a cast iron one. Let mixture set for minutes on top of stove, and then bake in oven for approximately 20 minutes at 350 degrees until middle is done. Cool slightly and invert on large plate to serve.

Serves: 8

"Bon Apetite"

JIM LEHRER is best known for his role as co-host of the "MacNeil/Lehrer NewsHour." His recipe reflects the many years he worked in Texas before coming to Washington.

Jim Lehrer
North Texas Nachos

This is one of those flexible recipes where the amounts vary according to taste. The measurements given cover generously the contents of an 8 ounce bag of Doritos or other similar Nacho chips.

   2 cups chili, without beans
1- 1½ cups chopped white onions
   1 ½-2 cups grated cheddar, longhorn or colby cheese
   1 11¼-ounce jar jalepeno peppers

Appetizers

Spread plain Doritos or nacho chips on baking sheet. Cover with "gobs" of the remaining ingredients in the order listed.

Bake at 350 degrees for 6-8 minutes or until cheese bubbles.

Serves: 6

"Eat with fingers if possible, otherwise use fork. Serve with pitchers of draft Pearl beer."

FRANK HARDEN is the taller half of WMAL's morning team. He's been partners with Jackson Weaver for more than 25 years. Frank's wife Berit comes from Sweden and can attest to the authenticity of the recipe.

Frank Harden
"Inlagd Sill" (Pickled Herring)

- 4 fillets of Matjes herring (canned)
- 1 large red onion, sliced
- 10 black peppercorns, crushed
- 1 bay leaf
- 3-4 sprigs fresh dill, to taste
- 1 cup vinegar (approximate)
- ⅓ cup sugar
- 2 tablespoons dry sherry
- ¼ cup tomato catsup

Cut herring fillets in bite size pieces. Layer the herring, dill, peppercorns and sliced onion in a glass jar. Put in bay leaf. Mix remainder of ingredients and pour over herring mixture. Liquid should cover all other ingredients. If it does not, add more vinegar to cover herring mixture. Let stand at least overnight.

Serves: 6 or 8

Serve with your smorgasbord, with crisp Swedish bread and a pony of Aquavit. "Smakling Maltid and Skal!"

PAM SIMON is the director of the Broadcasters' Child Development Center.

Pam Simon
Salmon Dip, Spread, Log

- 1 16-ounce can salmon
- 8 ounces cream cheese, softened
- 1 tablespoon lemon juice
- ¼ teaspoon salt
- 2 tablespoons onions, finely diced
- ¼ teaspoon liquid smoke (optional)

To form into log:
- ½ cup chopped nuts
- 3 tablespoons snipped parsley

Drain and flake salmon, reserving one or two tablespoons of liquid. Remove skin and bones. Put in a small bowl and thoroughly mix the salmon with a fork until it is very finely flaked. Add softened cream cheese, lemon juice, salt, diced onions and liquid smoke.

Mix until very well blended with a fork. If mixture is too thick, add some of the reserved salmon liquid. Chill for several hours, overnight if possible.

Serve as dip with raw vegetables and crackers. It is also good as a sandwich spread on dark pumpernickel bread. The chilled salmon mixture can be shaped into a log or balls and then rolled in a mixture of nuts and parsley. Can be stored in refrigerator for 1 to 2 weeks.

Serves: 8

"Salmon Balls or Logs wrapped in clear plastic make nice gifts."

KATHY BYE is a parent at the Broadcasters' Child Development Center.

Kathy Bye
Shrimp Mousse

1½ tablespoons gelatin
¼ cup cold water
1 can tomato soup
3 3-ounce packages cream cheese
¾ cup mayonnaise
3 cups celery, finely chopped
¼ cup spanish onion, finely chopped
1 pound frozen small shrimp, thawed and dried

Soak gelatin in cold water. Heat soup to boiling. Dissolve cream cheese in soup, add gelatin and cool. Add mayonnaise, celery, chopped onion, and seasonings. Prepare a large mold pan by spraying with Pam, or coating well with oil. When mixture begins to thicken, pour a layer into mold, follow with a layer of shrimp. Continue alternating layers until both shrimp and soup mixture are all used. Place in refrigerator and chill until set.

Serves: 6-8

"This is best if prepared the day before and stored in refrigerator."

SUSAN LECHNER is the producer of "Pick Up The Beat," a children's music video program at WJLA-TV.

Susan Lechner
Hot Spinach Dip

4 tablespoons butter or margarine
1 small onion, minced
1 can cream of mushroom soup
4 ounces cheddar cheese, grated
1 10-ounce package frozen chopped spinach, thawed
  Garlic powder, to taste
  Salt and pepper

Saute onion in butter for five minutes. Add soup and cheese. Squeeze excess moisture from spinach and add the spinach to soup and cheese mixture. Stir to blend. Add a few shakes of garlic powder to taste. Simmer over low heat for 20 minutes. Stir occasionally. Season with salt and pepper as needed. Serve in chafing dish with king size corn chips.

Serves: 4-6

"This is very easy and always gets high ratings."

HOLLY FINE is a producer and editor for "CBS Reports" and "60 Minutes." Before joining CBS, she worked for several years at WJLA. She is a former president of the Washington Chapter of N.A.T.A.S. and a founding parent of the Broadcasters' Child Development Center.

Holly Fine
Spinach Dip in a Loaf

- 2 10-ounce packages chopped frozen spinach, thawed and drained
- 2 cups mayonnaise
- ½ cup sour cream
- 3-4 scallions, chopped
- 1-2 teaspoons garlic powder
-   Salt and pepper to taste
- 1 loaf Italian bread, unsliced

Mix together spinach, mayonnaise, sour cream, scallions, garlic powder, salt and pepper. Cross slice loaf of bread about ¾ of the way through, leaving bottom uncut. Scoop out the center slices, leaving a two inch rim all the way around the loaf. Fill loaf with mixture. Use bread slices for dipping, and when they are used up, just pull apart sides of loaf already presoaked with dip.

Serves: 6-8

HENRY TENENBAUM joined WRC in 1982. He is the station's medical reporter and host of a weekly program on health topics. He's been a familiar face to Washington viewers since 1974 when he joined WTOP-TV (now WDVM-TV) as a reporter, and later as host of Channel 9's "PM Magazine." Before coming to Washington, Henry worked in Buffalo, New York.

Henry Tenenbaum
Steak for the Sushi Lover (Steak Tartare)

- 1 teaspoon salt
- 1 teaspoon pepper
- ½ teaspoon fresh parsley, chopped
- ½ onion, very finely chopped (optional)
- 1 teaspoon capers, drained
- 1 teaspoon wine vinegar
- 1 teaspoon catsup
- ½ teaspoon tabasco sauce, to taste
- 1 teaspoon lemon juice
- 6 drops garlic juice
- 2 egg yolks, lightly beaten
- 1 pound very lean ground round steak
- 1 teaspoon dill, chopped
- Toast wedges

Blend salt, pepper, parsley, onion, garlic juice, capers, wine vinegar, catsup, tabasco sauce, lemon juice and mix well. Add egg yolks. Add steak and regress into your childhood by kneading the whole mixture with your hands. After it is kneaded and mixed well, sprinkle dill on top. Invite two or three understanding friends to share with you on toast wedges.

Serves: 3-4

Note: Henry submitted a similar recipe three years ago when the cookbook project first started. When he resubmitted it this year it was in the format above. How have Henry's eating habits changed in three years? Well, he's cut the amounts of mustard, tabasco, onion and garlic in half. And he is now using toast wedges instead of his hands to eat the mixture!

TIM O'BRIEN is law correspondent for ABC News.

Tim O'Brien
Artichoke Soup

8 ounces artichoke hearts, in brine
3 cups chicken broth
8 ounces light (table) cream
3 onions, chopped

2 ounces butter
1 teaspoon flour
White pepper to taste
Chopped pimentos to taste (optional)

Saute onions in butter, set aside.

Cook artichokes in chicken broth for 25 minutes. Mix in blender. If artichokes are tough, soup may be strained. Add cream, onions and flour. Season with white pepper to taste. Pimentos may be added if desired.

Serves: 4-6

"This soup is fast and good."

GAIL FLANNIGAN is producer and director for WJLA specials and documentaries.

Gail Flannigan
Third Quarter Black Bean Soup

- 1 cup olive oil
- 3 cups yellow onions, diced
- 8 garlic cloves, crushed
- 2 pounds black turtle beans, soaked overnight
- 1 ham bone (with some meat)
- 5-6 quarts water
- 2 tablespoons cumin seed
- 1 tablespoon dried oregano
- 3 bay leaves
- Salt to taste
- 2 teaspoons freshly ground pepper
- Pinch of cayenne pepper
- 6 tablespoons parsley, chopped
- 1 sweet red pepper, diced
- ¼ cup dry sherry
- 1 tablespoon brown sugar
- 1 tablespoon lemon juice
- 1 cup sour cream

Heat oil in large kettle. Add onions and garlic and cook over low heat until tender. Drain beans and add to onions and garlic. Add ham bone and water. Stir in seasonings, reserving half of parsley. Bring to boil, reduce heat and cook, uncovered for about 1½ hours or until beans are tender and liquid is reduced by about ¾ths. Remove ham bone and cool slightly. Pull off any remaining meat and return meat to soup. Stir in remaining parsley, red pepper, sherry, brown sugar and lemon juice. Simmer for approximately 30 minutes. Serve very hot garnished with sour cream.

Serves: 8-10

"Sunday afternoons are the only time I have enough time to really mess up the kitchen. During the football season, if the Redskins are behind in the third quarter and I can't bear to keep watching, I retreat to the kitchen. This recipe was adapted from one of my favorite cookbooks, 'The Silver Palate.' It is a real winner no matter what happens on the field."

JACQUILINE GALES is a show producer for WDVM's "Carol Randolph Show."

Jacquiline Gales
Working with a Cold Chicken Soup

- 6 skinned and boneless chicken breasts
- 6 boullion chicken cubes
- ½ head cabbage, cut in large pieces
- 2 stalks celery, cut in large pieces
- 2 carrots, cut in large pieces
- Garlic cloves, minced, to taste
- ½ onion
- Red pepper, to taste
- Tumeric, to taste
- Paprika, to taste
- 1 tablespoon butter
- Parsley, to taste
- Salt
- Anything else mom used to put in

Boil water in large pan, add chicken breasts and boullion cubes. Reduce heat

Appetizers

and simmer at medium heat for 20 minutes. Add cabbage, carrots and other ingredients gradually. Let simmer over low heat for approximately 2 hours.

Serves: 4 for one day, or
       1 for three days

"This is a meal you can enjoy for the rest of the week or at least until your cold goes away. If you fix it on Sunday and get tired of it by Monday, add lentils or beans simmer slowly until new ingredients are cooked . . . voila, a new dish."

JEFF BOSTIC is a regular commentator for WTTG and WMAL radio. And in his spare time is a center for the Washington Redskins. As an original "Hog," he is known for his love of food.

Jeff Bostic
Clam Chowder

  1 medium potato, diced
  1 large celery stalk, diced
  ¼ cup onions, chopped
  1 6½-ounce can clams, with juice
  4 tablespoons butter
  ¼ cup flour
  1¼ tablespoons mixed salt & pepper, to taste
  ⅛ tablespoon sugar
  2⅔ cups milk
  ⅓ cup sour cream

Simmer vegetables in clam juice about 10 minutes until soft. While this mixture is cooking make white sauce with butter, flour, milk, salt & pepper mixture, and sugar. Cook over medium heat. Stir in vegetables and clams and juice. Just before serving stir in sour cream and heat over low heat.

Serves: 6

KATHY BYE is a parent at the Broadcasters' Child Development Center.

Kathy Bye
Cream of Carrot Soup

- 2 tablespoons butter
- ½ cup onion, coarsely chopped
- 1 pound carrots, peeled and quartered
- 1 pound potatoes (3 large), peeled and quartered
- 6 cups chicken broth
- 2 teaspoons thyme
- 1 bay leaf
- ¼ teaspoon sugar
- ½ teaspoon Worcestershire sauce
- Dash tabasco
- Salt and pepper to taste
- 1 cup heavy cream, or Half and Half
- 1 cup cold milk

In large pot, heat butter and add onions. Cook until slightly glazed and golden, stirring occasionally. Add carrots, potatoes and chicken broth. Bring to boil. Add thyme, bay leaf, sugar, worcestershire sauce, tabasco. Reduce heat and simmer 30-40 minutes or until vegetables are tender. Add salt and pepper to taste. Let cool.

Puree with heavy cream and milk. Serve chilled or reheat over low temperature to serve warm.

Serves: 6-8

LAUREN WERNER is a videotape editor for WDVM's Eyewitness News. She enjoys experimenting with new recipes whenever she is not hunting for antiques.

Lauren Werner
The Best Cucumber Soup

- 4 medium cucumbers
- 6 tablespoons butter
- ½ cup onion, chopped
- 10 chicken bouillon cubes
- 2 teaspoons wine vinegar
- 1 teaspoon dill weed
- Dash cayenne
- Dash paprika
- 4 tablespoons white cornmeal
- 2 tablespoons parsley
- 4 cups water
- 3 cups plain yogurt or sour cream
- Milk (optional)

Seed and chop cucumbers into ½ inch chunks. Melt butter in heavy saucepan, stir in onions and cook over medium heat for one minute. Add cucumbers, reserving a few pieces for garnish, water, bouillon cubes, vinegar, dill, cayenne and paprika. Bring to boil, add more water if it does not cover cucumbers, add cornmeal. Simmer uncovered for 20 minutes. Put mixture in a blender or processor and puree slightly. Add salt and pepper to taste. Chill thoroughly. Before serving, add sour cream and/or yogurt. Add milk, if desired, to adjust consistency to suit taste. Garnish with parsley and cucumber slices. Serve cold.

Serves: 8

"You can mix yogurt and sour cream together for a total of 3 cups to suit your taste."

IRVING R. LEVINE is a veteran NBC news correspondent. He is currently the network's chief economic correspondent.

Irving R. Levine
Easy and Good Gazpacho

- ½ cucumber, peeled and seeded
- ½ red onion, peeled
- ½ teaspoon oregano
- 3 tablespoons olive oil
- 2 tablespoons wine vinegar
- 4 cups Libby's tomato juice
  Salt to taste
- ½ avocado
  Juice from ½ lime

Dice cucumber and onion. Mix with oregano, olive oil, vinegar, tomato juice and salt. Stir well and refrigerate for a few hours or overnight. Before serving, peel and thinly slice avocado and sprinkle with juice from ½ lime.

To serve, put 2 ice cubes in each bowl. Add the soup and garnish with avocado slices.

Serves: 6

BARBARA GRUNBAUM is the government production coordinator for Montgomery Community Television.

Barbara Grunbaum
Delicious & Simple Gazpacho

- 1 28-ounce can tomatoes with juice
- 2 clove garlic, crushed
- 1 green pepper
- 3 tablespoons vegetable oil
- 2 tablespoons vinegar
- ½ teaspoon cumin seed
- 2 slices bread
- 3-4 slices, cucumber
- 1 pint water

Mix all ingredients together in blender and chill before serving.

Serves: 4

SUSAN LAINE is news information coordinator for ABC News in Washington. Before joining ABC, she worked for WJLA-TV.

Susan Laine
Gloria's Lentil Soup

- ½ cup vegetable oil
- 3 cups cooked ham, diced
- ½ pound polish sausage, cut in ½ inch slices
- 2 large onions, finely chopped
- 1 clove garlic, crushed
- 2 cups celery, chopped
- 1 cup carrots, chopped
- 1 large tomato, peeled and cut in wedges
- 1 pound lentils, washed
- ½ teaspoon tabasco sauce
- 1½ teaspoons salt
- 1 10-ounce package frozen chopped spinach
- 6 cups water

In large kettle, heat oil, add ham, sausage, onion and garlic and cook for 5 minutes. Add celery, carrots, tomato, lentils, tabasco, salt and water. Cover and cook over low heat for 2 hours. Add spinach and cook 10 minutes.

Serves: 8

"I stole this recipe from my best friend. I always double the recipe because it is always such a hit. If you double the recipe, you only have to increase the lentils to 1¼ pounds. It is a meal in itself with a loaf of good bread. You can add a hambone for extra flavor, too."

Appetizers

GENA FITZGERALD is a producer for News 7's investigative unit. She has worked at WJLA since 1978. When she isn't digging up stories, she is doing volunteer work with the Alexandria Urban Archeology Program.

Gena Fitzgerald
Mom's Pasta Fazool (Pasta and Bean Soup)

- 2 large cloves garlic
- 1 large onion, minced
- ½ cup celery, chopped
- 2 teaspoons dried basil
- 1 teaspoon oregano
- ¼ cup olive oil
- 1 20-ounce can white kidney beans with liquid
- 1 carrot, sliced in rounds
- 1 28-ounce can crushed tomatoes
- ½ pound tubettini style pasta
- Fresh grated cheese, to taste
- Salt and pepper

Heat oil in frying pan. Saute garlic, onion, celery, basil and oregano. Simmer until onions are soft. Add crushed tomatoes and any liquid from can. Simmer until well mixed. Transfer tomato mixture to large soup pot. Add carrots and beans, crushing just a few of the beans against the side of the pot to help it thicken. Let the soup simmer on low heat for about one hour. If the soup gets too thick, you can add a cup of chicken or beef broth. Meanwhile, in a separate pot, bring salted water to boil. Add the tubettini, cooking until it is just done and firm to bite. Be sure not to overcook it or it will get mushy when added to soup. When pasta is done, drain in colander and set aside. After soup has cooked, add pre-cooked tubettini, and cook just until heated through.

Serve with fresh grated cheese, and salt and pepper to taste.

Add a salad and warm Italian bread for a delicious and simple dinner.

Serves: 8

"This is an old family favorite that has been handed down through several generations. In a pinch, you can use red kidney beans instead of white, . . . but please don't tell my mother I told you to do that!"

ELLEN KINGSLEY is WDVM-TV's consumer reporter. She joined the Eyewitness News staff in 1980 after working as a consumer reporter for WJZ in Baltimore.

Ellen Kingsley
All Purpose Salad Dressing

- ½ cup vinegar
- ¼ cup sunflower oil
- 1 teaspoon Vegit (a "no salt" salt substitute available at health food stores)
- ½ teaspoon garlic powder
- 2 tablespoons fresh dill, chopped
- 2 tablespoons fresh Italian parsley
- ¼ cup blue cheese (optional)

Combine vinegar and oil. Add Vegit, garlic powder, chopped dill and parsley. Beat vigorously with a fork or whisk. If using blue cheese, crumble into mixture and mix thoroughly. Flavor to taste with additional Vegit.

Serves: 4-6

"This is a fairly low-salt, low-fat recipe, but blue cheese adds both salt and fat.

MIMI WEYFORTH DAWSON is a Federal Communications Commissioner appointed in 1981. She represents the FCC in matters of national defense. Before her appointment, she served as chief of staff to Senator Bob Packwood and on other Congressional staffs.

Mimi Weyforth Dawson
Celery Seed Dressing

- 4 cups salad oil
- 1 small onion, grated
- 1 tablespoon celery seed
- 2 tablespoons dry mustard
- 2 tablespoons salt
- 2 cups sugar
- 1⅓ cups cider vinegar

Mix oil, onion, celery seed, mustard, and salt. Set aside.

In a saucepan, add sugar to vinegar and bring to boil. Reduce heat and add other ingredients. Beat until it reaches desired thickness. It will become thicker the longer you heat it. Remove from heat and chill well.

"This will keep for months in the refrigerator. It is delicious served over Boston bib lettuce and Mandarin oranges."

MARLENE SHIPPY-KOEBBE is the administrative assistant for Montgomery Community Television.

Marlene Shippy-Koebbe
Leon's Secret Sauce

- 1 cup salad dressing
- ¾ cup chili sauce
- 1 tablespoon sweet pickle relish
- Dash Worcestershire sauce
- Garlic salt, to taste
- Salt and pepper, to taste

Mix all ingredients together and chill well.

Serves: 6-8

"This is a family favorite that beats any store-bought Thousand Island dressing."

MADELINE LaCORE is a segment producer for WDVM-TV's "Capital Edition" program.

Madeline LaCore
Auntie's Salad

- 1½ tablespoons honey
- ¼ cup mayonnaise
- 4 or 5 cups cabbage, shredded
- 4 medium carrots, shredded
- 1 large Delicious apple (or 2 medium)
- ½ cup seedless raisins
- ½ cup white raisins

Mix honey and mayonnaise. Set aside. Core and dice apple, but do not peel. Mix cabbage, apples, raisins and carrots. Toss ingredients well and mix with honey and mayonnaise mixture. Serve cold or at room temperature.

Serves: 4-6

Appetizers

JOHN MURPHY is the morning drive personality on WBMW-FM.

John Murphy
Chicken-Apricot Salad

- ¼ cup mayonnaise
- ¼ cup sour cream
- 1 cup yogurt (optional)
- 2 tablespoons lemon juice
- 1½ tablespoons tarragon mustard
- 1½ cups dried apricots, diced
- 4 cups cooked chicken, diced
- 1 cup celery or water chestnuts, chopped
- 1 teaspoon salt

Blend mayonnaise, sour cream, yogurt, lemon juice, mustard and salt in large bowl. Add apricots, chicken, and celery or water chestnuts. Toss lightly, combine all ingredients well. Refrigerate overnight in tightly covered container. Serve in a croissant or on bed of lettuce garnished with additional chopped apricots.

Serves: 4-6

KATY WINN RITZENBERG is a parent at the Broadcasters' Child Development Center.

Katy Winn Ritzenberg
Cucumber and Yogurt Salad

- 1 large cucumber
- ¾ cup plain yogurt
- ¼ cup sour cream
- 1 clove garlic, chopped
- Vinegar to taste
- Dash of chive or chopped green onion, optional

Slice cucumber and place in bowl. Add remaining ingredients and mix lightly. Serve plain or on bed of lettuce.

Serves: 2-3

KATHY BYE is a parent at the Broadcasters' Child Development Center.

Kathy Bye
Fresh Spinach and Strawberry Salad

- 1 pound fresh spinach
- 1 pint fresh strawberries
- Poppy seeds for garnish

Salad Dressing:
- 2 tablespoons dijon mustard
- 2 tablespoons honey
- 2 tablespoons olive oil
- ½ cup vegetable oil
- 2 tablespoons red wine vinegar

Wash and drain spinach and strawberries. Toss together and set aside. Blend salad dressing ingredients well. Immediately before serving, pour salad dressing over spinach and strawberry mixture and garnish with poppy seeds.

Serves: 8

"This is very good."

JAN BROWN McCRACKEN is a parent at the Broadcasters' Child Development Center.

Jan Brown McCracken
Frosty Strawberry Salad

- 8 ounces strawberry yogurt
- ¼ cup sugar
- 8¾ ounces fruit cocktail, drained
- 2 tablespoons chopped pecans

Mix all ingredients together. Put into small molds or muffin cups. Freeze. Remove from freezer immediately before serving.

Serves: 6

CAROL RANDOLPH is host of WDVM-TV's "Carol Randolph Show." Carol, who has been with Channel 9 since 1969 is a former high school biology teacher and a lawyer who specialized in Communications.

Carol Randolph
Layered Lettuce Salad

- 1 small head lettuce
- 1 cup celery, diced
- 4 hard boiled eggs, sliced
- 1 10-ounce package frozen peas, uncooked
- ½ cup green pepper, diced
- 1 small onion, diced
- 8 slices bacon, cooked and crumbled
- 2 cups Miracle Whip salad dressing
- 2 tablespoons sugar
- 4 ounces cheddar cheese, grated

Tear lettuce into bite size pieces and place at bottom of glass dish. Add remaining ingredients in layers, in the following order: celery, hard boiled eggs, peas, green pepper, onion. Add sugar to Miracle Whip and place on top like frosting. You can add the bacon now or wait until serving. Top with cheese and refrigerate for at least 12 hours. Toss when ready to serve. If you've waited to add bacon, sprinkle on top immediately before serving.

Serves: 12

"I find the bacon becomes limp if added before refrigerating. I recommend adding it after chilling."

SCOTT KLUG is a reporter with WJLA-TV's investigative unit. TESS KLUG is operations manager for WETA. They are parents at the Broadcasters' Child Development Center.

Scott and Tess Klug
Sesame Seed Salad

- 1 bunch green onions, chopped
- 1 large head leaf lettuce
- 1 cup chow mein noodles
- 4 tablespoons sesame seeds
- 3 ounces slivered almonds, toasted

Dressing:
- ½ cup oil
- ½ cup sugar
- 6 tablespoons vinegar
- 1 teaspoon salt
- 2 teaspoons Accent
- ½ teaspoon ground black pepper

Mix ingredients for dressing and refrigerate.

Toast almonds at 350 for 15 minutes. Chop onions, wash and drain lettuce. Combine and toss onions, lettuce, noodles, sesame seeds and almonds. When ready to serve, pour on dressing.

Serves: 4-6

"The dressing makes this salad!"

JAN THOMPSON is senior producer and segment host for WDVM's "Capital Edition." Before joining WDVM in 1983, she worked as a reporter and anchor in Cincinnati.

Jan Thompson
Tri Color Pasta Salad

- 2 pounds fresh tri-color pasta
- 1 green pepper
- 1 red pepper
- ⅓ pound provolone cheese
- ¼ pound hard salami
- 1 12-ounce can pitted black olives, sliced
- ¼ pound pepperoni

Dressing
- ½ -1 cup olive oil (approximate)
- ¼ -½ cup red wine vinegar (approximate)
- ⅓ small onion
- 1-2 cloves fresh garlic, crushed
- ½ teaspoon tarragon
- 1 teaspoon basil
- Salt and pepper to taste

Cook fresh pasta in boiling water approximately 5 minutes until al dente. Rinse in cold water. While pasta is cooking, slice salami, pepperoni, peppers and cheese into strips approximately 1½ inches long and ½ inch wide. Combine with noodles. Add olives. Coat with dressing. Add salt and pepper to taste. Marinate in refrigerator overnight, stirring occasionally.

<u>Dressing</u>: You can use any homemade or bottled dressing you prefer, but if you want to use the one Jan uses, combine the above ingredients, mixing well before pouring over pasta mixture.

Serves: 8

MARK SEEGER is news production manager for WDVM's Eyewitness News. An employee of Channel 9 since 1969, he has worked as assignment manager and as ENG producer. He is also a parent at the Broadcasters' Child Development Center.

Mark Seeger
Tuna Salad Supreme

- 2   6½-ounce cans tuna, packed in water
- 5   hard cooked eggs
- 6   medium stalks celery, finely chopped
- 1   small onion, finely chopped
- 6-7 small sweet gerkin pickles, finely chopped or
  3 tablespoons sweet pickle relish
- 1 -1½ cups mayonnaise (approximate)

Drain and crumble tuna in large bowl. Chop eggs and add to tuna mixture. Add chopped celery, chopped onion and pickles or pickle relish. Stir in mayonnaise, adjusting amount to suit taste. Chill well. Serve on bed of lettuce with crackers. It also makes great sandwiches.

Serves: 4-6

"This is a lunchtime favorite at our house. If you make it the night before, the flavors blend nicely."

MAINCOURSES

SARALEE TODD is a parent at the Broadcasters' Child Development Center.

Saralee Todd
Beef Brisket

3-4 pounds beef brisket, first cut
1 large onion, sliced
½ bottle Italian salad dressing
½ cup catsup
   Garlic powder, to taste
   Paprika, to taste
½ cup or more wine (optional)
2 tablespoons flour, or more as needed for pan juices

Place brisket fat side down in large baking dish. Rub with garlic powder and paprika. Turn brisket fat side up and rub again with garlic powder and paprika. Put sliced onion around, over, and under brisket.

In a separate bowl, mix salad dressing, catsup, and wine (optional). (Note: you may vary the amount depending on the size of brisket.) Pour over brisket and cover tightly with aluminum foil. Bake in a 325 degree oven; approximately 3 hours for a 3-4 pound brisket.

When done, place brisket on cutting board. Slice fat from top and discard. Slice brisket, *against the grain.*

Take as much pan juice as desired from the baking dish and pour into small pan. Mix flour with a small amount of water, and stir well to blend. Add to juices, stirring constantly over medium heat until thickened. Return brisket to baking dish, and serve with gravy.

Serves: 6-8

"This tastes great as leftovers & makes terrific sandwiches."

DAVE THOMSON was with Q107 when he submitted this recipe back when the cookbook project first started.

Dave Thomson
Beef Burgundy

- 3 pounds round steak, cut into bite size pieces
- 2 cans cream of mushroom soup
- 1 package dry onion soup mix
- 1 cup Burgundy wine
- 1 4-ounce can mushrooms

Put steak into casserole dish. Mix the soups with the wine until well blended. Add undrained mushrooms to the wine-soup mix, and stir well. Cover and bake for 2 hours at 350 degrees or until meat is fork tender.

Serves: 6-8 generously.

"Serve over rice, egg noodles, or wild rice. Excellent!"

DAN LEWIS is a news anchor and reporter for WJLA-TV.

Dan Lewis
Beef Choufleur (Beef & Cauliflower)

- 1 pound boneless round steak, cut ⅓ inch thick
- 1 small head cauliflower
- 2 tablespoons butter
- 1 green pepper, cut in ¾ inch pieces
- ¼ cup soy sauce
- 1 clove garlic, minced
- 2 tablespoons cornstarch
- 1½ cups beef broth
- 1 cup green onions, sliced
- 3 cups cooked hot rice

Cut meat in ½ inch cubes. Separate cauliflower into flowerettes. Brown meat in butter about five minutes. Add cauliflower, green peppers, soy sauce and garlic. Stir lightly to coat vegetables with soy sauce. Cover pan and simmer until vegetables are barely tender, about 10 minutes. In a separate bowl, blend cornstarch and beef broth. Add to mixture along with green onions. Cook, stirring constantly, until thoroughly heated and sauce is thickened. Serve over beds of fluffy rice.

Serves: 6

"Believe me, this is much better than the Hamburger Helper recipes I labored over in college. Now the truth . . . I never made this. It is my wife Patty's recipe."

CAROLE MARCHESANO is president of Goldberg, Marchesano and Associates.

Carole Marchesano
Beef and Radishes Stir Fry

- 2 tablespoons oil, or more as needed
- ½ pound flank steak, sliced thin and in small pieces
- 1½ cup radishes, sliced crosswise
- ¼ cup green onion, chopped in ¼" pieces
- 1 teaspoon cornstarch
- 2 tablespoons soy sauce

Sweet/Sour Sauce:
- ⅓ cup vinegar
- 4 tablespoons water
- ½ cup sugar
- 1 tablespoon cornstarch

Mix cornstarch and soy sauce and set aside.

Mix sweet/sour sauce and set aside. Smear meat with soy/cornstarch mixture. Heat wok, adding oil. Saute meat for a minute, then remove. Pour in sweet/sour sauce and stir for a second. Add radishes, mixing well with sauce and cook about 3 minutes. Add onion, cooking 1 minute. Add meat, and cook a minute or so. Serve as is or over rice.

Serves: 4

JIM CLARKE is an investigative reporter for News 7. He has been with WJLA since 1962.

Jim Clarke
Beef Wellington

- 1 box frozen puff pastry patty shells
- 2½ to 3 pounds filet of beef
- 2 teaspoons brandy
- Salt and pepper, to taste
- 6 slices bacon
- 1 egg, beaten

Defrost patty shells several hours ahead, following directions on box.

Preheat oven to 325 degrees. Place beef on rack in shallow pan, basting with brandy. Place bacon across top of filet. Cook 12 minutes *per pound*. Remove from oven and cool to room temperature. Remove bacon.

Preheat oven to 425 degrees.

Roll pastry until thin. Place pastry over beef, covering it. Trim and tuck edges, carefully eliminating any double thickness. Brush with beaten egg. Make slits in pastry with knife. Bake in oven for 30 minutes, then enjoy.

Serves: 6

JOEL LOY co-hosts WTTG's "PM Magazine". Before joining Channel 5, Joel worked in Rochester, New York.

Joel Loy
Braised Beef with Polenta

- 2 pounds lean stew meat, cubed
- Flour, as needed
- 2 tablespoons olive oil
- 1 medium onion, chopped
- 1 clove garlic, chopped
- 4 ounces mushrooms, sliced
- 1 cup water
- 1 15-ounce can marinara sauce (can use *Ragu*)
- ½ cup sherry or red wine
- ½ teaspoon Italian seasoning
- Salt and pepper to taste

Dredge meat with flour. Saute meat, onion, and garlic with olive oil in large, heavy skillet until meat is browned. Add remaining ingredients. Cover and simmer gently, stirring frequently, for about 2 hours. If needed, add a little more water as sauce cooks down.

Polenta

1½ cups cornmeal
1½ teaspoons salt
4½ cups water
¼ -½ pound cheddar cheese, shredded
3 tablespoons butter

Mix cornmeal, salt, and 1½ cups cold water on top of double boiler. Stir in 3 cups boiling water. Cook over low heat, stirring occasionally til thickened. Cover, cook for 45 minutes, stirring occasionally. Add cheese and butter, stirring until they are melted and blended. Add more salt if needed to taste. To serve, spoon in a ring onto a heated platter. Fill center with braised beef.

Serves: 4-6

"Polenta is a wonderful substitute for potatoes or rice. An Italian specialty, it can also be chilled overnight . . . then sliced and fried. This is my favorite recipe."

GEORGIA ORPHAN is a senior designer with WJLA-TV.

Georgia Orphan
TV Designer Beef Curry

1 pound lean ground beef
3 tablespoons peanut or vegetable oil
1 tablespoon curry powder
½ teaspoon salt
¼ teaspoon pepper
1 clove garlic, finely chopped
  Chopped mushrooms, to taste
½ cup onion, cut in ½ inch pieces
3 tablespoons soy sauce
1 cup boiling water
3 teaspoons cornstarch mixed with 6 tablespoons water

Place curry in frying pan over medium heat. Stir 3 minutes. Add oil, garlic, salt and pepper. Brown beef in oil/curry mixture for 5 minutes. Add soy sauce, mushrooms, onions and boiling water and boil 2 to 3 minutes. Add cornstarch/water mixture to beef and stir over heat until thickened.

Serve over rice with chutney, ground peanuts and whatever else appeals.

Serves: 4-6

"Fast and cheap."

GORDON BARNES has been WDVM's chief meteorologist and weathercaster since 1976. He began working in the weather business at age 16 and has been the meteorologist for "CBS Morning" with Charles Kuralt, the CBS radio network and WCBS-TV. He operates a weather forecasting service to radio stations and businesses.

Gordon Barnes
Bermuda Breakfast

> Bacon
> Eggplant, sliced
> Bananas
> Eggs
> Raisin Bread
> Cold Beer

Fry bacon . . . keep bacon grease in frying pan. Remove bacon, then simmer eggplants and banana in frying pan.

Prepare eggs as desired, and can fry them in bacon grease if desired.
Toast raisin bread. Serve with beer, good and cold.

Serves: 1

"Good luck."

Note: *This is one of those recipes where the amounts are up to the individual and can be adjusted to suit your own taste.*

GLENN HARNDEN teaches film and video production at The American University.

Glenn Harnden
Black Beans and Rice

- 2 16-ounce bags black beans (red beans can be substituted)
- 1½ to 4 pounds beef (chuck roast, round, oxtail, etc.)
- 7-8 medium onions, chopped
- 7-8 cloves garlic, sliced
- ⅔ cup lemon juice
- Pepper, to taste
- Salt, to taste
- Celery salt, to taste
- Thyme, to taste
- 2-3 cups beef bouillon (preferably Spice Islands Beef Stock)

Soak beans overnight until rejuvenated (about 6-8 hours). Chop up beef and saute in oil or in its own fat. Add in onions, garlic, stock and lemon juice. Add the beans and simmer for about four hours, until the beans are tender and the beef is broken down. Serve over rice with hot green chile sauce.

Serves: "4 people for 3 days"

"Toward end of cooking, or when reheating, add some pork, or Polish sausage, or whatever!"

Maincourses

JOHN CORCORAN submitted this recipe back when this cookbook project first began and he was at WJLA working as a reporter and critic. He now works in Los Angeles.

John Corcoran
Cork's Caloric Tripledecker

3-4 slices Velveeta or similar processed cheese
　　Peanut butter, crunchy or smooth
1 ripe banana
3 slices white bread
　　Mayonnaise

　　On one slice of bread, place several thick slices of cheese. Then put a light layering of mayonnaise. Apply the second slice of bread. On top of that, put a good slathering of peanut butter. Be careful, so you don't tear bread. Slice banana to desired thickness, and apply directly to peanut butter. It should stick in place nicely. Slather a good dose of mayonnaise on top of banana. Place third slice of bread directly on top. Slice sandwich and eat.

Serves: 1

"As you can tell, cooking isn't my forte, but in the interest of the project, here is a recipe you can use. It is good with a light burgundy or good California chablis."

Note: By all reports, John really eats this.

GINGER MIELKE worked as a producer in WJLA-TV's Public Affairs Department. She now works for Rep. Michael Barnes.

Ginger Mielke
Your Choice Broccoli Casserole

- 1 10-ounce package frozen chopped broccoli
- 1 cup cooked long grain rice
- 1 small onion, diced
- 1 tablespoon vegetable oil
- ½ - ¾ cup celery, diced
- 1 can cream of mushroom soup
- 1 small jar Cheese Whiz
- ¼ cup milk
- 1½ cups of one of the following: cubed cooked chicken, cubed cooked ham, peeled and cooked shrimp, or cleaned crab.

Cook broccoli according to package directions and drain well. Saute onion and celery in oil. In large bowl, mix all ingredients together and pour into greased 2 quart casserole. Bake 30 minutes at 350 degrees or microwave for 6-8 minutes, until hot and bubbly throughout.

Serves: 6

"This recipe can be made a day or so in advance. It freezes well and can be doubled easily to serve a crowd."

WILLARD SCOTT is best known as the zany "Today Show" weatherman. But before joining the NBC show, he spent many years in Washington as weatherman for WRC-TV and as part of the popular "Joy Boys" radio team. He also has the distinction of selling fresh eggs to fellow employees at WRC . . . eggs which he transported with care from his farm in Virginia.

Willard Scott
Cheese Grits Souffle

- 1 cup quick cooking grits
- 4½ cups water
- 1 teaspoon salt
- 6 tablespoons butter
- 1 stick Kraft's Garlic (optional on the garlic) Cheese
- 2 beaten eggs
- ¼ cup milk
- Salt and pepper
- 1 cup crushed corn flakes
- 2 tablespoons butter

Cook grits in water with 1 teaspoon salt. When done, stir in 6 tablespoons butter and the cheese. Allow to cool. Add beaten eggs and milk to grit mixture. Season with salt and pepper. Pour into buttered casserole dish and cover with corn flakes mixed with 2 tablespoons butter. Cover well. Bake 40-44 minutes at 350 degrees F.

Serves: 6

"DELICIOUS!!!"

SAMARA MARTIN is a show producer for WDVM's "The Carol Randolph Show."

Samara Martin
Cheese and Onion Pie

　10　inch pie crust, unbaked
　10　ounces Swiss and/or gruyere cheese, grated
　　2　tablespoons flour
　　2　large onions, chopped
　　4　tablespoons butter
　　1　teaspoon chopped basil
　　2　large tomatoes, sliced
　　2　large eggs
　¾　cup cream or Half and Half
　　　Ground nutmeg, to taste

Preheat oven to 350 degrees.

Toss grated cheese with flour.

Melt butter in large skillet and saute onions very gently until they begin to turn golden, about 30 minutes. Spread about ⅓ of the cheese over the bottom of pie crust. Spread onions on top of cheese. In the butter that is left in pan, heat tomato slices and basil for a few minutes. Arrange tomato slices over the onions in pie pan. Cover with remaining cheese.

In a medium bowl, beat eggs with cream and pour over cheese-onion mixture. Sprinkle with ground nutmeg. Bake for 35-40 minutes or until top is golden brown. Serve hot in wedges.

Serves: 6

"This is a favorite of mine adapted from the 'Vegetarian Epicure'."

Maincourses

MIKE LEWIS is the voice of Channel 9. As staff announcer for WDVM-TV, his voice is heard on news opens, station promos and I.D.'s. He also has a wide range of national credits as writer, producer and talent on radio and TV spots. He readily admits that his wife Susan didn't marry him for his cooking.

Mike Lewis
Chicken Breasts with Sesame Seeds

1½ tablespoons white wine vinegar
1½ tablespoons dry sherry
 1 tablespoon reduced sodium soy sauce
 2 large chicken breast halves, skinned and boned
1½ tablespoons sesame seeds
1½ tablespoons corn oil

Combine vinegar, sherry, and soy sauce. Place breast in mixture and freeze, if desired. Otherwise, marinate breasts several hours or overnight. If breasts are frozen, defrost before next step. Remove breasts from marinade and dip in sesame seeds. Brown in hot oil on both sides.

Add marinade; cover and continue cooking until breasts are cooked through, 7-10 minutes.

Double the marinade for three or four chicken breasts.

Serves: 2

TOM JARRIEL is a correspondent with ABC News, a regular contributor to "20/20" and a weekend anchor for ABC.

Tom Jarriel
Chicken-Broccoli Casserole

6-8 chicken breast halves
2 10-ounce packages frozen broccoli spears, cooked

Sauce
2 cans cream of chicken soup
1 cup mayonnaise
3 teaspoons lemon juice
1 cup sharp cheese, grated
1 teaspoon Worcestershire sauce

Boil chicken breast, then skin and bone. Butter a flat baking dish. Put broccoli on bottom, place chicken over broccoli. Blend well ingredients for sauce, then spoon over chicken & broccoli. Bake at 350 degrees for 35-40 minutes.

Serves: 6

"This freezes well and is easily halved to serve two or three."

Maincourses

DICK DYSZEL is better known to the children of Washington as "Captain 20," Washington's longest running children's show host. He is known to their parents as "Count Gore De Vol," long time host of Creature Feature.

Dick Dyszel
Chicken-Cheese Roll Supreme

- ¼ teaspoon flavor enhancer
- 2 whole breasts, cut from 2 broiler-fryer chickens
- 3 cups Mazola corn oil
- 1 can cream of onion soup
- 10 ¾ ounces French Columbard wine
- 1 teaspoon ground pepper
- 1 tablespoon grated parmesan or romano cheese
- ½ teaspoon paprika
- 1 teaspoon garlic salt
- ½ teaspoon salt
- ⅓ cup flour
- 4 ounces monterey jack brick cheese
- ⅓ pound fresh mushrooms, sliced
- 1½ cups cooked rice

Bone, skin, and halve breasts, then flatten. Preheat corn oil to 375 degrees. Stir together in medium bowl: flour, garlic salt, pepper, and grated cheese. Sprinkle flavor enhancer over the inside portion of each breast half. Slice brick cheese into thin, narrow strips. Place ¼ of these strips on the inside portion of each breast half and roll jellyroll style with top of breast on the outside. Dredge in

Combine the can of soup with 10¾ ounces (one soup can) wine. Add 2 tablespoons of flour mixture and salt. Stir until smooth and pour sauce over chicken rolls in casserole. Add mushroom pieces and sprinkle paprika over the chicken rolls. Microwave uncovered for 7 minutes and serve on a bed of rice.

Serves: 4

Note: If your microwave doesn't have a turntable, it is best to turn the dish halfway through the cooking time.

DEBORAH TALLEY is a director for ABC News in Washington. Prior to joining ABC, she worked at WJLA.

Deborah Talley
Diet Delight Chicken

- 4 boneless chicken breasts
- ⅔ cup unsweetened pineapple juice
- ⅓ cup soy sauce

Remove skins from chicken breasts. Mix pineapple juice with soy sauce. Marinate chicken for 1 hour. Broil chicken breasts on each side and baste with sauce. Serve with 2 tablespoons of sauce poured over breasts.

Serves: 4

"I was served this recipe while vacationing at a Phoenix Spa. It's great and easy, too."

JEAN HABTEAB is an administrative assistant with WJLA-TV.

Jean Habteab
Doro Wat (Ethiopian Chicken Stew)

- 1 whole chicken
- 3 large yellow onions
- 4 large white potatoes, peeled and quartered
- ½ pound collard greens
- 2-3 medium tomatoes, peeled
- 1 green pepper, diced
- Red ground pepper or cayenne pepper, to taste
- 2-3 hard cooked eggs (optional)
- 1 6-ounce can tomato paste (optional)
- ¼ cup flour (optional—for thickness)

Remove skin from chicken. Soak ½ to 1 hour in water with one onion that has been halved. This gives flavor to the chicken. For added flavor, run onion directly onto chicken.

Tear fresh greens into 2-3 inch pieces. Place chicken, potatoes, greens, tomatoes, onions, green pepper in 6-8 quart pan with enough water to cover ingredients. Bring this mixture to boil and cook for 45 minutes. Simmer for additional 10 minutes.

Tomato paste and/or flour can be added for thickness. Add red pepper to taste. Ethiopian dishes are traditionally very, very hot. Whole boiled eggs are added after other ingredients have thoroughly cooked.

Serves: 4-6

"This stew is traditionally eaten with a bread like enjera, but you can substitute pita bread for this. Hot tea with cinnamon stick is a good beverage to serve with this. Dessert is not traditional with Ethiopian meals."

Note: You can substitute frozen greens for fresh greens, but they should be thawed and drained and added near the end of the cooking time.

SHARMAN MESARD is a freelance associate director with both CBS & ABC News.

Sharman Mesard
Chicken Divan

3-4 pounds chicken breasts or parts
3 cups fresh broccoli, chopped
2 cans cream of chicken soup
1 cup mayonnaise
1 tablespoon curry powder (or more to taste)
1 cup cheddar cheese, grated
1 cup bread crumbs
1 tablespoon butter, melted

Cook and slice chicken. Cook broccoli until tender; drain. Arrange broccoli in casserole dish or in 11½ × 7½ × 1½ inch pan. Place chicken on top of broccoli. Combine soup, mayonnaise, curry powder, and cheese. Pour over chicken and broccoli. Combine bread crumbs and butter—sprinkle over casserole. Bake for 25-30 minutes at 350 degrees.

Serves: 4-6

"I prefer cheddar cheese, but you can substitute other types. And, I more than double the amount of curry powder."

JACK SMITH is a principal reporter for ABC News' "This Week with David Brinkley." Jack, the son of newsman Howard K. Smith, joined ABC in 1976.

Jack Smith
The Chicken of Forty Garlics

- 40 small to medium cloves of garlic
- 6 chicken quarters (more, if needed)
- 6 large onions, sliced
- 3 medium eggplants, sliced
- 3 medium squash, sliced
- Butter, as needed (or olive oil)
- Salt and pepper, to taste
- ¼ cup chicken broth
- ¼ cup white wine or vermouth
- Flour and water paste

Preheat oven to 400 degrees. You'll need a large, ovenproof pot with cover, and saute pans.

Brown chicken over medium-medium high heat and salt to taste. Do the same with the eggplant and squash. Brown onions very lightly. Save the liquid from the chicken, eggplant, etc.

Layer in ovenproof pot: chicken, then sprinkle garlic cloves, then squash and eggplant, then sprinkle more garlic cloves, then more chicken, and continue until pot is full.

Reduce liquid in saute pan. Add wine or vermouth, chicken broth and salt. Pour into pot with chicken-garlic mixture. Add pats of butter, or oil, as needed, to pot.

With flour and water, make a paste. Apply the paste to rim of pot. Place lid on top, making it air-tight. Put in oven. Remove after 15 minutes . . . checking paste around rim for leaks, patching if necessary.

Lower oven to 350 degrees. Cook for 2½ to 3 hours, depending on amount of chicken in pot. Serve with toast . . . separating garlic and smearing it on toast. Juice will be very rich—pour over servings.

Serves: 5-6

"Chicken of 40 Garlics is a literal translation from the French, but don't worry, it's not garlicky at all. It originates from Southern France & Northwestern Italy."

GLORIA FAVA is the cook for WDVM-TV's general manager.

Gloria Fava
Chicken Gloria

  4 boneless chicken breasts
     Salt and pepper, to taste
  4 tablespoons melted butter
  1 orange
  1 lemon
  1 cup sour cream
  ½ pound mushrooms
  ½ cup dry white wine or sherry
     Parsley

Season the chicken breast with salt and pepper. Brown in a skillet. Put the chicken in an ovenproof dish. Add melted butter, orange peel, lemon peel, and some of the juice from both fruits. Bake for 30 minutes at 350 degrees. Remove from oven and add the sour cream, mushrooms, and wine. Bake an additional 10 minutes. When ready, sprinkle with chopped parsley and serve.

Serves: 4-6

DAVE FOXX can be heard on WCLY "Classy 95" Radio.

Dave Foxx
Chicken Juicy

- 1 3-3½ pound chicken
- 8 tablespoons butter
- 1 tablespoon garlic salt

Melt butter and add garlic salt. Mix well. Cut chicken in serving-size pieces. Throw fresh chicken on grill without any additional seasoning. Start basting with butter sauce. The secret is to use low heat and turn the chicken pieces often, basting every time you turn the chicken. When you run out of butter, the chicken should be golden brown, juicy and delicious. Caution: Keep a spray bottle of water handy to keep the coals from flaming too much.

Serves: 4-6

"This barbeque concoction is extremely simple, but it gets rave reviews every time I serve it."

PATRICK ELLIS is a producer and announcer with WHUR-FM. He hosted a cooking show on WHUR in the late 70's and used this recipe on his first show.

Patrick Ellis
Chicken Pelau (Trinidad)

- 2 packages of chicken thighs, *approximately 3 pounds*
- Garlic salt
- Black pepper
- Hot pepper sauce
- Thyme
- 1 medium onion
- Celery
- 3 teaspoons vegetable oil
- 2 teaspoons brown sugar
- 5 cups water
- 8 ounces coconut creme
- 3 cups rice (uncooked)
- 1 can pigeon peas
- 3 cups raisins

TV Dinners

Cut chicken off the bone and dice into bite-size pieces. Season meat with spices and herbs (to your taste). Chop onion and celery; add to chicken. Heat oil and brown sugar until sugar burns. (It should turn black and smoke.) Pour sugar and oil mixture into a deep cooking pot; add chicken mixture, turning frequently to brown. After chicken is well-browned, add only *one* cup of water and cook over medium flame until chicken is *half* done. Blend in coconut creme; add four cups water and the rice; cook over medium flame until rice is almost done. Add pigeon peas and raisins. Cover and simmer until most of water has cooked off the rice.

Serves: 6-8

"Don't worry if you get a little burning on the bottom of the pot. This is called the 'bun, bun' in the islands, and some say it's the best part of the dish."

STEVE HAGEDORN writes and produces promo's for WDCA-TV.

Steve Hagedorn
Chicken and Sausage Skillet

- 1 teaspoon olive oil
- 4 pounds frying chicken (cut up)
- Salt and pepper to taste
- 1 pound Italian sausage
- 1 cup chopped onion
- 1 cup sliced mushrooms
- 1 cup sliced green pepper
- 1-2 cloves garlic
- 1 teaspoon oregano
- 1 can (28 ounces) Italian tomatoes
- ½ cup chicken stock
- 1 cup white wine

Heat olive oil. Brown chicken, adding salt and pepper to taste. Prick skin of sausage, adding to chicken. Brown for 15 minutes and drain off fat.

Maincourses

Add onion, mushrooms, green pepper, and sliced garlic. Add oregano. Cover with tomatoes, stock, and wine. Stir to loosen bits at bottom of pan. Cover tightly and simmer 20 minutes. Serve over rice or spaghetti.

Serves: 4-6

"When cooking with wine, always use a wine you would drink and use equal proportions for the recipe and the chef."

RENEE ANTOSH is an account executive at WTTG and a parent at the Broadcasters' Child Development Center.

Renee Antosh
Chicken Shrimp Supreme

- ¼ cup butter
- ½ pound sliced fresh mushrooms
- 2 tablespoons sliced onion
- 2 cans (10½ ounces each) cream of chicken soup
- ½ cup sherry
- ½ cup light cream or Half and Half
- 1 cup cheddar cheese, shredded
- 2 cups cooked chicken, cut up
- 2 cups cooked shrimp
- 2 tablespoons parsley

In a 3 quart saucepan, melt butter. Add mushrooms and onion, saute five minutes. Add soup; gradually stir in sherry and cream. Add cheese and heat over low heat, stirring occasionally until cheese is melted.

Add chicken and shrimp. Heat to serving temperature but do not boil. Just before serving, stir in parsley. Serve with hot buttered rice.

Serves: 3-4

"Very good!"

LaGERIS BELL is associate producer with the WDVM documentary unit.

LaGeris Bell
Afro-Dite Barbequed Chicken

- 1 3-4 pound chicken
- 2 -3 cloves garlic, minced
- 1 large onion, chopped
- ¼ to ½ cup honey
- 1 teaspoon parsley
- ½ teaspoon sage
- ½ teaspoon thyme
- 1 teaspoon pepper
- ½ cup teriyaki sauce
- 2 cups peanut or olive oil
- 1 32-ounce can tomato sauce
- 1 6-ounce can tomato paste
- ¼ cup vinegar
- ⅓ cup mustard

Combine minced garlic, chopped onion and honey. Let stand overnight at room temperature. Mix herbs, teriyaki sauce and oil. Marinate chicken in herb/teriyaki sauce for 3-4 hours. Drain oil from chicken. Mix together tomato sauce, tomato paste, vinegar and mustard. Pour over chicken and marinate 3-4 hours more. When ready to cook, drain any extra oil from chicken and add garlic-honey mixture. Coat chicken well. Bake uncovered for 2 hours at 350 degrees.

Serves: 4-6

"All amounts are guestimates to suit my taste. Please adjust amounts to suit yours."

GORDON PETERSON is Eyewitness News anchorman at 6 p.m. and 11 p.m. He joined WDVM-TV (then WTOP-TV) in 1969. In addition to his anchor duties, he continues to work as writer, producer and reporter on series and specials. Prior to coming to Washington, he worked as a journalist in Boston.

Gordon Peterson
Gordon's Chinese Chicken

- 2 boneless chicken breasts
- 2 sweet red peppers
- 1 hot pepper (optional)
  A few spring onions
  Soy sauce, to taste
  Duck sauce, to taste
  Cornstarch, for thickening
  Oil
  Slivered almonds

Take the chicken breasts and remove skin (yuk!). Semi-freeze it, then cut it into bite-size chunks. Take a couple of red peppers. Chop them up. You want spicy, chop up a hot pepper. Otherwise, forget it. Chop up some spring onions. Take some soy sauce, some duck sauce, some cornstarch, some oil. Mix it up with the chicken in a dish for a while. Throw the whole thing into a hot, well-greased wok. Stir-fry. Throw some slivered almonds in there. Do not overcook the chicken or it will be tough. Serve with rice.

Serves: "One very large hungry person" or "3 or 4 small not-so-hungry persons."

"If your guests throw the chicken back at you, I guess I left something out. If not, I guess it's o.k."

Note: Amounts will vary according to taste and size of chicken, but chicken should be lightly coated with the cornstarch, soy sauce mixture. We've given you Gordon's directions just as he gave them to us.

BETSY and JOE HART are parents at the Broadcasters' Child Development Center.

The Hart Family
Breasts of Chicken with Cream

- 4 tablespoons butter
- 6 halves chicken breasts, skinned and boned
- ½ teaspoon lemon juice
- ½ cup bouillon
- ½ cup Madiera or dry white vermouth
- 1 cup whipping cream
  Pinches of garlic, nutmeg, salt, pepper, paprika
  Flour, if needed

Maincourses

Melt butter in ovenproof casserole until foamy. Add chicken breast, lemon juice, salt and pepper . . . saute for 4-5 minutes on each side. Remove chicken. Add bouillon and wine to casserole and boil down liquid until syrupy. Stir in cream and boil down again. (If liquid is too watery, add flour as needed to thicken.) Add garlic, nutmeg and paprika. Pour over chicken and serve with rice.

Serves: 4-6

"This is a Julia Child recipe as adapted by the Hart family."

JIM ELLIOTT is half of the popular Elliott and Woodside team at Q107. The team, together since 1978, joined Q107 in 1982. He has also worked at WPGC and WRC radio. He is a native of New York.

Jim Elliott
Easy Chicken Casserole

- 4 chicken breasts (or 1 whole chicken, cut up)
- 1 cup mushrooms, sliced
- 1 can cream of mushroom soup
- ½ cup sour cream
- 1 teaspoon Worcestershire sauce
- 2 tablespoons Heinz 57 sauce or catsup
- 1 teaspoon tarragon
  Dash of salt and pepper
- 1 teaspoon parsley

TV Dinners

Combine all ingredients, except chicken and parsley. Arrange chicken in ovenproof casserole. Pour mushroom sauce over chicken. Sprinkle with parsley. Cover and bake in 350 degree oven for 35-45 minutes, depending on amount of chicken. We take it out when the sauce gets very brown around the edges. Use extra sauce to pour over white rice as a side dish.

This recipe may also be baked in a crock-pot on high for 3-4 hours. Note: omit the sour cream until the last half-hour of cooking if using this method.

Serves: 4-5

SUSAN KING is a news anchor for Channel 4's 6 p.m. newscast. Her "Susan King's Cover Story" airs nightly on the 11 p.m. newscast. Before joining WRC-TV in 1983, she worked as a correspondent for ABC News and as a reporter and anchor for WDVM-TV. Before coming to Washington, she worked in television in New York City and in Buffalo, New York.

Susan King
Emmies Chicken

- 8 cooked and diced chicken breasts
- 1 cup chopped celery
- 1 cup almonds, chopped
- French Dressing, to coat (preferably Good Seasons Riviera French)
- Grated cheddar cheese, to taste
- 1 cup mayonnaise
- 1 can French fried onions, optional

Marinate diced chicken overnight in French dressing. Use just enough dressing to coat the chicken . . . don't let it get saturated.

In mixing bowl, add celery and almonds to chopped chicken. Mix well with mayonnaise as if making a cold chicken salad.

Put the mixture into a baking dish, and generously add cheddar cheese over the top. Bake 30 minutes or until thoroughly heated at 325 degrees. If you decide to add the French fried onions, sprinkle on top of cheese and heat another five minutes. Serve warm with a salad and French bread.

Serves: 8

"This is a recipe originally served to 150 after an Emmy awards ceremony, so this is really named after us!"

DIANA PUMPHREY is the administrative assistant to the News Director at WTTG-TV.

Diana (Clark) Pumphrey
Hawaiian Chicken

- 1 package each: chicken legs, thighs, & breasts (about 3 pounds)
- 1 6-ounce can of frozen orange juice
- 2 tablespoons butter
- 1½ cups crushed pineapple
- 3 teaspoons ginger, to taste
- 3 teaspoons soy sauce, to taste
- 3 cups cooked rice

Pre-heat oven to 375 degrees. Put chicken in large pan. Mix pineapple and orange juice in bowl. Melt butter, then add to juice mixture. Add ginger and soy sauce (to suit taste). The mixture should be a light brown color. Pour juice mixture over chicken and put into oven for about an hour, or until chicken is done. Cook rice separately and use the juice mixture from pan as a sauce. Add a salad and rolls and it's a dinner.

Serves: 4-6

"It's easy and almost like a casserole, all cooked in one pan except the rice."

SANDRA SOUTHERLAND is WHMM-TV's assistant to the technical operations manager.

Sandra Southerland
Italian Chicken

1½ pounds chicken, cut up
 ½ cup onions, sliced
 ½ cup green pepper, sliced
 4 cups spaghetti sauce (or more as needed)
 1 teaspoon parsley
 1 tablespoon oregano
 ¼ cup white wine
 1 clove garlic, chopped or crushed

Combine chicken, white wine, onions, green pepper, garlic, parsley, and oregano. Bake at 350 degrees for one hour. Pour spaghetti sauce over chicken, and bake for 30-45 minutes more or until chicken is done. Can serve over spaghetti, or with stir-fried zuchinni, green peppers, and onions.

Serves: 4

MARGE KUMAKI is a news reporter and anchor for WMAL radio. She is also a parent at the Broadcasters' Child Development Center.

Marge Kumaki
Lollipop Chicken

- 2 packages chicken wings (about 24 wings)
- 1 cup cornstarch
- Garlic salt, to taste
- Oil, as needed, for frying
- 2 eggs, beaten

Dipping Sauce:
- ¾ cup sugar
- ½ cup vinegar
- 2 tablespoons ketchup
- 1 teaspoon soy sauce
- 1 teaspoon salt
- ½ cup chicken stock (or water)

Separate chicken wings (save the tips to use for chicken stock or in another recipe). Sprinkle garlic salt on wing pieces and refrigerate for a few hours or overnight.

For dipping sauce: simmer ingredients together in saucepan until all sugar has melted. Use wire whisk for best results in blending ingredients together.

Dip chicken pieces in cornstarch and then in beaten egg. Fry wings until crisp. Immediately after frying, dip each piece in sauce and then place on baking sheet. After each wing has been fried and dipped, bake for 30 minutes at 350 degrees. If desired, sauce can be heated and put on table for more dipping.

VIVIAN BURCH is an administrative assistant for Eyewitness News at WDVM-TV. Over the years, her co-workers at channel 9 have come to admire her work as a great cook.

Vivian Burch
Quickie Gourmet Chicken

- 4 boneless chicken breasts
- 1 cup mushrooms, chopped
- ½ cup bread crumbs
- ½ teaspoon pepper
- 1 slice swiss cheese, divided into four pieces
- 1 cup white wine
- 1 package filo dough, prepared according to package directions

Preheat oven to 350 degrees. Saute mushrooms and seasonings in butter. Add wine, and cook until wine evaporates. Remove and cool slightly.

Add bread crumbs and swiss cheese to mushroom mixture. Stuff mixture between folded chicken breasts. Wrap each stuffed chicken breast in one sheet of filo dough (following package instructions). Bake 40-45 minutes at 350 degrees.

Serves: 4

"Great served with wild rice and a green vegetable of your choice."

DEBRA SILIMEO is a news reporter and anchor for WTOP radio. She has also worked at WRC-TV.

Debra Silimeo
Raspberry Chicken

- 4 chicken breasts
- ½ cup sherry
- 1 10-ounce package frozen raspberries
- ½ teaspoon thyme
- 1 fresh lime

Defrost raspberries and mix with sherry, thyme and juice from ½ lime. Arrange chicken breasts in ovenproof pan and spoon sauce over chicken. Bake for approximately 30 minutes at 350 degrees. As chicken cooks, spoon sauce over chicken to keep it moist. Serve topped with slices of fresh lime.

Serves: 4

"This dish is really simple to make. You can bake it as above, or broil it if you're short on time, but the sauce doesn't stand up as well if broiled. Either way, it is great served with wild rice and broccoli."

KAROLYN MIXON is Special Projects Coordinator for WHMM-TV.

Karolyn Mixon
Schlemmertoph Chicken (Chicken in a Clay Pot)

- 1 chicken, cut in parts (or 1 package assorted parts)
- 4 potatoes, peeled
- 6 carrots, peeled
- 2 whole onions
- ½ to 1 pound string beans, optional
- 1 tablespoon worcestershire sauce
- ½ teaspoon garlic salt
- Salt and pepper to taste
- ½ teaspoon paprika

Soak (Schlemmertoph) clay pot in cold water for 15 minutes. Set aside and let dry. Season chicken with salt, pepper, paprika and garlic salt. Place chicken in pot. Cut vegetables in good sized pieces, cut onions in quarters. Place all around pot and sprinkle with worcestershire sauce. Cover with top and place in cold oven. Set oven for 375 degrees. Bake for one hour.

Serves: 4

"Natural juices from chicken will cook vegetables, resulting in a steam in pot. No basting is necessary."

ANGELA ROBINSON is a general assignment reporter with WTTG. She has worked at Channel 5 since 1983. She worked in Atlanta before coming to Washington.

Angela Robinson
Southern Fried Chicken

6-8 pieces chicken
  Nature's Seasoning Salt
1 -1½ cups buttermilk
  Fresh ground pepper
1 -1½ cups flour
  Vegetable oil or shortening for frying

Sprinkle with Nature's Seasoning Salt. Place in bowl and cover with buttermilk. Let chicken stand in buttermilk for several minutes. Mix black pepper with flour. Roll chicken in flour mixture. Fry in hot oil or fat until deep golden brown and crispy.

Serves: 6

"Great served with potato salad."

Maincourses

JUDY HUBERT is the head infant teacher at Broadcasters' Child Development Center.

Judy Hubert
Southern Fried Chicken

6-8 pieces fresh chicken
1 cup flour
 McCormick Season Salt, to taste
1 cup vegetable oil

Wash chicken, pat dry. Sprinkle season salt on chicken. Put chicken in refrigerator for 2-3 hours or overnight to let flavor go through chicken. Sprinkle season salt in flour and mix with fork. Coat chicken with seasoned flour. Heat vegetable oil in 10 inch skillet until oil is very hot. Put chicken in hot oil and brown on one side for about 30 minutes. Turn chicken over, cooking other side until golden brown.

Serves: 6

GARY MURPHY works at the Voice of America. When he submitted this recipe, he was at Q107.

Gary Murphy
Chili

1 pound ground beef	1 tablespoon sugar
1 medium onion	1 teaspoon salt
2 cans light red kidney beans (drained)	1 teaspoon pepper
1 large can of tomato juice	Dash of cayenne pepper
1 tablespoon chili powder	Pinch of green bell pepper flakes

Break up and brown ground beef (drain grease), chop and saute onion. Combine all ingredients in a large pot and let simmer uncovered over low heat for 3 hours. The longer it cooks the thicker it gets. Stir occasionally.

Serves: 4 hearty appetites

"This chili recipe is quick, easy, inexpensive and delicious on cold winter days. Serve with tossed green salad, crackers and bread."

TV Dinners

MORRIS JONES is a general assignment reporter and anchor of the weekend newscasts. He joined Channel 5 in 1983 and has a wide range of interests including computer technology.

Morris Jones
Chili with Pinto Beans and Venison

- 2 cups fresh pinto beans
- 2 pounds venison meat, cut in cubes or
  2 pounds ground beef
- 2 8-ounce cans tomato sauce
- 1 6-ounce can tomato paste
- 2 4-ounce cans chopped green chiles
- 1 cup onions, chopped
- 1 12-ounce can beer
- Salt and pepper to taste
- Pinch of cumin

Fry venison meat or ground beef and drain off excess grease. In a large heavy pot, combine meat with remaining ingredients and simmer for 1 hour.

Serves: 8

"I'm from the West and love my raw meat. But it still works if you use ground beef. The beer adds a great taste to the chili."

JOHN LYON is co-host of "The Lyon and Walker Show" for WMAL radio. He joined WMAL in 1967 and has been in broadcasting for over 25 years including work as a weatherman and talk show host. A native of Illinois, he has worked there and in Ohio before coming to Washington. John is a talented folk and bluegrass guitarist and plays in a local group.

John Lyon
Festival Chili

- 3 tablespoons lard, butter or bacon drippings
- 2 large onions, coarsely chopped
- 8 pounds beef, chuck or round, coarse ground (chili grind)
- 5 tablespoons plus 1 teaspoon hot red chile, ground
- 5 tablespoons plus 1 teaspoon mild red chile, ground
- 1 tablespoon dried oregano
- 3 8-ounce cans tomato sauce
- 3 cups water

Melt the lard, butter or drippings in a large, heavy pot over medium heat. Add onions and cook until translucent. Combine the beef with the garlic, ground chile, cumin and oregano. Add meat and spice mixture to onions. Break up any lumps and cook, stirring occasionally until evenly brown, about 30 minutes. Add tomato sauce and water. Bring to boil, lower heat and simmer for at least 1 hour. Taste and adjust seasonings to taste.

Serves: 16

"Don't forget the cold Mexican beer!"

FRANK HERZOG is WJLA's sports director and host of "The John Riggins Show." He is also heard during football season on WMAL radio as part of the team that brings viewers the Redskins games. Before joining Channel 7, Frank worked as a sportscaster for WDVM-TV and for WTOP radio. Frank's chili recipe is well known among his friends and gets rave reviews from them.

Frank Herzog
Frank's Standard American Chili

   Bacon grease
1 medium onion, chopped
1 clove garlic, minced
1 bay leaf
1 20-ounce can cooking tomatoes
2 52-ounce cans Hanover Redskin kidney beans
3½ -4 pounds lean ground beef
2 -3½ tablespoons McCormick Mexican-style hot chili powder

In dutch oven, brown chopped onion and garlic in bacon grease. Add ground beef, cooking until browned. Cut up canned tomatoes, add to mixture and simmer. Sprinkle on chili powder beginning with 2 tablespoons and increasing to suit taste. Dump in kidney beans, one of them partially drained. Stir.

Finally, add bay leaf, submerging slowly into the brew. Meanwhile, have a family member or close personal friend read the first six verses of the poem "Hiawatha." (Any Indian-sounding verse may be substituted.) Sprinkle on a little salt. Cook over low heat, stirring occasionally for at least 4 hours. If, after 2

Maincourses

hours, your brew looks like nothing more than hamburger, beans and some tomatoes, you're doing perfectly.

If "Hiawatha" was read with any feeling at all, your chili should be ready 5 hours after you began. If possible, let it cool overnight in the garage and re-heat for a taste thrill.

Serves: A crowd

"Chili should be served with chopped onions, shredded sharp cheddar cheese, chili peppers and toastado chips. To avoid gas, eat the chili with toastado chips only. This stuff reacts to the metal in spoons."

RICH ADAMS is editorial director for WDVM-TV where he has worked for 14 years. In addition to his current position, he has worked as assistant news director and reporter for Channel 9. Rich also worked for NPR, Voice of America and in his native Minnesota. He is a registered emergency technician and active in the Bethesda Chevy-Chase Rescue Squad.

Rich Adams
Rescue Squad Chili

    3 pounds lean ground beef
    2 16-ounce cans peeled tomatoes
    2 16-ounce cans kidney beans
    2 medium onions, sliced or grated
 1-3 packages Texas 3 Alarm Chili Mix
    2 green peppers, chopped (optional)

Brown ground beef in large skillet. Pour drippings into large pot. Set meat aside. Put all other ingredients in kettle and mix well. Add 1 to 2 cups of water.

Bring to boil, stirring frequently. Reduce heat and simmer. Add meat and cook for 30 to 45 minutes or until slightly thick. If too thin, add more beans and meat.

Serves: A family, a firehouse or small country depending on quantity served.

"This recipe can be expanded or reduced easily."

ARCH CAMPBELL is WRC-TV's movie and theater critic and host of "The Arch Campbell Show." Arch joined Channel 4 in 1974 as a feature reporter and for a brief time provided weekend weather reports for Channel 4 News. A native of Texas, he has worked in Dallas as a radio announcer and as a news reporter.

Arch Campbell
"Real" Chili

- 3 pounds of the sorriest meat you can buy, stew meat coarse ground or, if you must, ground chuck
- 1 tablespoon oregano
- 1 tablespoon cumin seed, crushed
- 1 tablespoon salt
- 1 tablespoon powdered cayenne
- 1 tablespoon tabasco sauce
- 2 cloves garlic, chopped or mashed
- 3 tablespoons chili powder
- 2 heaping tablespoons Masa Harina

Sear meat in a large skillet or pot. Cover with 2 inches of water, and if using stew meat, simmer for 30 minutes.

Mix in remaining ingredients except for Masa Harina and bring to a boil, reduce heat and simmer for 45 minutes. Then take off stove, skim off grease and mix in Masa Harina. Simmer for 30 minutes. Let cook slightly and serve. It is actually better if you put it in the refrigerator overnight and serve the next day.

Serves: Approximately 10

"I grew up in Texas, where men are men and chili is chili, and beans are kept to the side and never put in the chili. If you want the real thing and have a cast iron mouth, you'll enjoy this recipe for Original Texas Chili. Very HOT, but terrific. 4 stars and 4 alarms."

Arch Campbell
Corn Bread for "Real" Chili

- 3 cups corn bread mix
- 2½ cups milk
- ½ cup vegetable oil
- 3 eggs, beaten
- 1 large onion, grated
- 3 tablespoons sugar
- 1 16-ounce can cream-style corn
- ½ cup jalapeno peppers, finely chopped
- 1½ cups cheddar cheese, grated
- 2 ounces crisp bacon, chopped
- ½ cup pimento, finely chopped
- 2-3 cloves garlic, chopped

Mix all ingredients until well blended. Bake approximately 30 minutes at 400 degrees.

"This is great if you really want to pig out with the chili. The recipe is like a corn quiche for 'real men.' Believe me, only a 'real man or woman' can eat this stuff, but the flavor is great."

JACKSON WEAVER had teamed up with Frank Harden to create the Harden and Weaver magic for more than 25 years on WMAL radio. Weaver began his broadcasting career in his hometown of Buffalo, New York and worked in New York, Pennsylvania and Ohio before joining WMAL in 1943. His voice is familiar to millions as that of "Smokey the Bear." He spends much of his free time on his tugboat "The Jack Tar."

Jackson Weaver
Jack Tar Crab Cakes

- 1 pound backfin or claw crabmeat
- 2 slices soft bread
- ½ cup milk
- 3 tablespoons mustard
- 3 tablespoons soft butter
- 2 eggs
- Dash of Old Bay Seasoning

Clean crabmeat and remove bits of shell. Soak and crumb bread. Mix with other ingredients. Mold into crabcakes. Fry until brown, or bake for 30 minutes at 350 degrees.

MARIA SHRIVER is co-anchor of the "CBS Morning News", and has spent much time living and working in Washington.

Maria Shriver
Maryland Crabcakes

- 1 pound crabmeat
- 1 teaspoon Old Bay Seasoning
- ¼ teaspoon salt
- 1 tablespoon mayonnaise
- 1 tablespoon worcestershire sauce
- 1 tablespoon chopped parsley
- 1 tablespoon baking powder
- 1 egg, beaten
- 2 slices bread, crust removed
- ¼ cup milk

For frying:
- 2 tablespoons butter
- 2 tablespoons vegetable oil

Break bread in small pieces and moisten with milk. Mix with other ingredients. Shape into cakes. Fry in mixture of 2 tablespoons butter and 2 tablespoons oil. Fry until golden brown, about 7 minutes on each side.

Serves: 4

SANDRA BUTLER is director of broadcast operations for WDVM-TV. She joined Channel 9 in 1980 as special projects producer after many years at WRC-TV.

Sandra Butler
Crab Imperial

- 1 teaspoon prepared mustard
- 4 tablespoons butter
- 2½ tablespoons mayonnaise
- 1 egg, beaten
- 1 pound back fin crabmeat
- 1 teaspoon chopped parsley
- ½- 1 cup buttered bread crumbs

Drain crabmeat and pick over to remove any shells. Set aside.

Mix mustard, butter, mayonnaise, egg and parsley together. Add crabmeat and mix gently. Sprinkle bread crumbs on top.

Bake for 30 minutes at 350 degrees.

Serves: 4

JEANNE BOWERS is a documentary producer for WDVM-TV.

Jeanne Bowers
Sauteed Soft Shell Crabs

- 12 soft shell crabs
- Flour for dredging
- Salt and pepper, to taste
- ½ cup butter
- ½ cup corn oil
- 2 lemons, cut in wedges

Dry the cleaned soft shell crabs on paper towels.

Dredge them with flour that has been seasoned with salt and pepper. Shake them off so that the flour coating is very light. Heat butter and oil together in heavy skillet. Saute crabs until they are light brown and crisp, turning to get both sides done evenly. Remove to hot platter, and serve with lemon wedges.

Serves: 4-6

"If you are serving die-hard crab lovers like me, it will only serve 4."

KAREN CAMPBELL works in the News Department of WHUR-FM.

Karen Campbell
Crab-Shrimp Bake

- 1 cup cooked cocktail shrimp
- 1 6½-ounce can crabmeat
- 1 cup celery, chopped
- ¼ cup green pepper, chopped
- 2 tablespoons onions, chopped
- ½ teaspoon salt
- Dash pepper
- 1 teaspoon worcestershire sauce
- ¾ cup mayonnaise or Miracle Whip
- Old Bay Seasoning, to taste
- 1 cup bread or cracker crumbs
- 1 tablespoon butter

Combine all ingredients and place in ovenproof dish. Melt butter and combine with crumbs. Sprinkle crumbs generously over shrimp/crab mixture. Bake for 30-35 minutes at 350 degrees.

Serves: 4-6

MARLENE SHIPPY-KOEBBE is administrative assistant at Montgomery Community Television.

Marlene Shippy-Koebbe
Doedoe's Poor-Do Casserole

- 1 pound all beef hotdogs
- 1 8-ounce can tomato sauce
- 1 cup water
- 1 large onion, chopped
- 1 tablespoon oil or margarine
- 2 cups shell or elbow macaroni
- Salt and pepper to taste

Cook macaroni according to package directions for al dente. Drain and set aside. While macaroni is cooking, saute onions in oil or margarine. Slice hot dogs and brown lightly in hot skillet. Combine onions, hot dogs, macaroni, tomato sauce and water in large saucepan and simmer 20-30 minutes until it begins to thicken.

Season to suit your taste.

Serves: 6-8

"This quick and easy dish is a favorite with both kids and adults."

PAUL SMITH works at WTTG and is former producer of "Newsbag" for Channel 5.

Paul Smith
Green Eggs and Ham in a Hat

- ¼ cup cooked ham, chopped
- 2 eggs
- Blue food coloring
- Salt and pepper to taste
- 1 slice bread

Combine chopped ham with 2 eggs, salt, pepper and several drops of blue food coloring. Whisk until frothy and evenly green. Cut a 2½ to 3 inch circle in the center of your favorite bread. A mayonnaise jar lid or cookie cutter works well. Place bread on greased skillet over medium heat. Pour egg mixture into center of bread. Cook until eggs are done, flip once, if desired.

Serves: 1

Note: You might expect a "green eggs and ham" recipe from a former children's show producer. This recipe is a hit with kids. For adults who aren't thrilled with eating green eggs, it works just fine without the food coloring.

FELIX GRANT has been heard on Washington radio for decades. He is currently heard on WRC radio and for many years was heard on WMAL radio.

Felix Grant
Feijoada

- 6 cups black beans
- 1½ pounds carne seca (dried beef)
- 1 pound Canadian bacon, or pork roll
- 1 pound beef sausage
- 1 pound Portuguese or Polish sausage
- Pepper and salt, to taste
- 1 tablespoon hot sauce or hot crushed pepper
- 2 large onions, whole
- 1 cup Manioc meal (farinha)
- 2 pounds collard greens
- 4 cups rice, cooked
- 4 medium oranges, sliced

Pick over beans, wash well, soak overnight in cold water. Soak dried beef, Canadian bacon and sausage overnight in cold water, each in a separate pan. Next day, drain the beans, place in a large pot with two whole onions. Add cold water and place lid on pot. Bring to boil, reduce heat to medium and cook for about 2 hours. Add water as needed to keep beans covered. Remove onions from pot after beans have cooked.

Drain dried beef, place in pot, cover with water and cook until tender, about 2 hours. Remove and cut into 1 inch cubes. Parboil Canadian bacon and sausages, and cut into bite-size pieces.

Add meat to beans and cook on medium heat until all meats are tender and beans are soft. Season with salt and pepper if needed. Add hot dried crushed pepper to suit taste.

Immediately before serving, transfer meat and bean mixture to large serving bowl. Heat Manioc meal in skillet or in oven until lightly brown and sprinkle over beans and meat when served.

Serves: 6-8

"FEIJOADA, pronounced fay-zwah-dah, is a Brazilian dish. Carne Seca and Farinha Mandioca can be purchased at food specialty stores. Serve with cooked collard greens, rice and orange slices."

R. RANDOLPH "RANDY" RITTER is a senior videotape technician at WTTG. He shares credit for this recipe with his wife Beth.

R. Randolph Ritter
Blue Cheese-Stuffed Flank Steak

½ pound blue cheese, chopped in small pieces
2½ -3 pounds flank steak
½ teaspoon or more ground black pepper
Salt, to taste

Preheat broiler.

Cut a pocket into the flank steak. Stuff an even, thin layer of blue cheese inside steak. Be sure to stuff pocket all the way back so the cheese is evenly distributed. Rub pepper into surface of steak, and salt to taste. Place under preheated broiler and cook 7 to 10 minutes on each side. Remove from oven, slice on diagonal and serve immediately.

Serves: 4

"This recipe came from the *Washington Post* and has become a favorite of ours for company and for just the two of us."

TAD DUKEHART is a news photographer at WDVM. He gives credit to his wife Andy for this recipe.

Tad Dukehart
Marinated Flank Steak

- 1 clove garlic (crushed)
- ¼ cup soy sauce
- 2 tablespoons cooking sherry
- 2 teaspoons honey
- 2½ -3 pounds flank steak

Combine ingredients and pour over flank steak. Marinate at least 2 hours, turning occasionally. Broil or grill on barbecue until done, approximately five minutes per side for rare, depending on thickness of steak.

Serves: 6

PATRICK ELLIS is a producer and announcer with WHUR-FM. He hosted a cooking show on WHUR back in the late 70's called "Patrick's Pantry."

Patrick Ellis
Stuffed Flounder

- ¼ cup chopped onion
- 4 tablespoons butter
- 1 3-ounce can chopped mushrooms, drained (save liquid)
- ½ pound backfin crab meat, drained and cartilege removed
- ½ cup coarse saltine cracker crumbs
- 2 tablespoons snipped parsley
- ½ teaspoon salt
- Dash pepper
- 2 pounds flounder fillets (8)
- 3 tablespoons butter
- 3 tablespoons flour
- ¼ teaspoon salt
- Milk
- ⅓ cup dry white wine
- 1 cup swiss cheese, shredded
- ½ teaspoon paprika

Preheat oven to 400 degrees. In skillet, cook onion in 4 tablespoons butter till tender but not brown. Stir drained mushrooms into skillet with flaked crab meat, cracker crumbs, parsley, ½ teaspoon salt and dash pepper. Spread mixture down the length of fillets and roll up like a jelly roll. Place rolled fillets down in a lightly oiled baking dish. In saucepan, melt 3 tablespoons butter. Blend in flour and ¼ teaspoon salt. Add enough milk to mushroom liquid to make 1½ cups, and add to pan. Add wine. Cook and stir over low flame until mixture thickens and bubbles. Pour over fillets. Bake for 25 minutes. Sprinkle with cheese and paprika; return to oven for 10 minutes longer or until fish flakes easily with fork.

Serves: 8

BILL MAYHUGH is one of those broadcasters whose day is turned around. His program has been heard on WMAL in the early morning hours since 1964 starting at 1 a.m. One of the originators of the Marine Corps Marathon, he is an avid runner and golfer. He also plays the drums and piano.

Bill Mayhugh
American Grilled Cheese Sandwich

- 2 slices white sandwich bread (square cut)
- 2 slices of good American cheese
- 1 slice large sweet onion
- 1 tablespoon butter
- Mustard & ketchup to taste

Heat skillet on low temperature. Place onion slice between the 2 cheese slices, and then between bread. Place pat of butter on each side of sandwich. Put in warm skillet . . . but do *not* press down on sandwich. When bottom is golden brown, flip sandwich. Again, do *not* press down on sandwich. When both sides are golden brown and just crisp, open sandwich gently . . . put small amount of mustard (preferably French's) and a thumb-nail of ketchup. Eat while it's still warm.

Serves: 1

"I like this best with French's mustard."

JOE HART is a parent at the Broadcasters' Child Development Center.

Joe Hart
French Toast

- 4 eggs
- ⅓ cup milk
- 1 tablespoon vanilla
- 1 teaspoon cinnamon
- 8-10 slices bread
- 2 tablespoons butter

Mix all ingredients together until well blended. Dip bread into mix until well soaked. Cook on buttered skillet until golden brown on each side.

Serves: 8-10

DAVE THOMSON was with Q107 when he submitted this recipe back when the cookbook project first started.

Dave Thomson
Ham and Egg Brunch

- 8 slices white bread, cubed, crusts removed
- 1 pound ham, cubed
- ¾ pound cheddar or american cheese, cubed
- 7-8 large eggs, lightly beaten
- 2¾ cups milk
- 1 teaspoon dry mustard
- 1¼ teaspoon salt
- 4 tablespoons butter or margarine, melted
- 1 tablespoon butter or margarine

Butter a 9 × 13 baking pan with one tablespoon butter. Place bread cubes and ham in pan. Top with cheese. Combine eggs and milk with mustard and salt.

Pour butter or margarine over top. Cover and refrigerate overnight. Bake, uncovered, 1 hour at 325 degrees.

Serves: 6-8 generous portions.

"Delicious!"

SUSAN FERTIG-DYKES is director of broadcast service for the Veterans Administration.

Susan Fertig-Dykes
Indonesian Curry Dinner

- 1 whole fresh chicken
- 1 pound lamb, cut in ½ inch cubes
- Salt and pepper, to taste
- ¼ cup flour
- 1 pound bacon
- 6-8 cups water
- 6 chicken bouillon cubes
- 4-5 large pieces celery, leaves intact
- 2-3 large carrots, cut in large pieces
- 2 large onions, quartered
- 1 teaspoon fresh parsley
- ½ teaspoon tarragon
- ¼ teaspoon cumin or corriander
- Handful of dry basil
- 1 large bay leaf, broken to release flavor
- 2 cloves garlic, minced
- 1 or 2 green apples
- 1 2-ounce bottle curry powder
- 1 teaspoon hot chili powder
- ½ teaspoon hot paprika

Cook bacon in large skillet. Reserve bacon fat to saute lamb and chicken. Set bacon aside for later use as condiment.

Dust lamb cubes with flour, salt, and pepper. Brown in bacon fat in large pot over high heat. Allow to cool slightly and then fill pot with 6-8 cups water. Bring to boil and simmer 1 hour or until lamb can be gently speared with fork. Add whole chicken, including neck, gizzards, and liver. Add bouillon cubes, vegetables, parsley, tarragon, cumin, basil, bay leaf and garlic and bring to boil. Simmer until chicken is tender. While chicken and lamb are simmering, take 1½ cups of the broth and use to poach diced apples until soft. Mash apples with fork and add approximately ½ can of curry, chili powder and paprika. Whip with fork and set aside.

Remove lamb and chicken from broth. Strain and reserve broth. Remove chicken from bones. Lightly flour lamb and chicken pieces and saute in bacon drippings in skillet.

Add apple-curry mixture, coating meat. Add strained broth and simmer until thickened, stirring only lightly to avoid shredding chicken.

Serves: 8

Serve with rice and assorted condiments placed on a lazy Susan or in small bowls on table. Suggested condiments include: chutney, chopped raw tomatoes, diced raw onions, chopped celery, raisins, shredded coconut, chopped peanuts, diced bananas, bacon bits, diced cucumbers, plain yogurt.

FRANCES STACHOW SEEGER is a producer at WJLA-TV. She was program acquisition manager for Montgomery Community TV. She worked at WTTG for several years and was producer of Channel 5's "Panorama." She is a parent at the Broadcasters' Child Development Center.

Frances Stachow Seeger
Never Fail Lasagna

- 1 pound lasagna noodles, prepared according to package directions
- 1½ pounds lean ground beef
- 1 medium sized yellow onion, chopped
- 2 cloves garlic, minced
- 1 teaspoon oregano
- 1 32-ounce jar Prego spaghetti sauce
- 5 eggs, beaten
- 1 cup parmesan cheese, grated
- 1 32-ounce container ricotta cheese
- 1 12-ounce container small curd cottage cheese
- 8 ounces mozzarella cheese, grated

Saute meat, onion and garlic until meat is brown. If necessary, drain off excess fat. Combine meat mixture, spaghetti sauce and oregano and cook over low heat for 15-20 minutes. While this is simmering, cook lasagna noodles according to package directions. Also prepare cheese filling by combining eggs, ½ cup of the parmesan, ricotta, cottage cheese and mozzarella. To assemble lasagna, place a layer of sauce in bottom of oblong baking dish and top with a layer of noodles, followed by a cheese filling, a layer of noodles, a layer of meat sauce, repeat, noodles, cheese, noodles, meat sauce. End with a layer of meat sauce. On top of sauce, arrange 4 or 5 tablespoons of cheese mixture equally spaced over entire baking dish. Sprinkle remaining ½ cup of parmesan cheese. Bake for 35-40 minutes at 375 degrees. Remove from oven and let stand for 20 minutes before serving.

Serves: 8-10

"I used to take the time . . . before kids and a house . . . to carefully prepare my mother's homemade spaghetti sauce recipe from scratch to use in the lasagna. While nothing is ever a match, I find that Prego or other thick sauces work fine. This recipe freezes well and tastes great reheated. Depending on the size of your baking dish and how generous you are with the filling, you might have enough to make a second dish of lasagne from one recipe."

PEYTON LIVELY is an engineering assistant at WHMM-TV.

Payton Lively
Seafood Lasagna

- 1 pound shrimp
- 1 pound lasagna noodles, prepared according to package directions
- 4 ounces ricotta cheese
- 2 eggs
- ½ cup onions or scallions, chopped
- ½ pound mushrooms, sliced
-   Old Bay seasoning, to taste
- 1 pound crab meat
- ½ pound flounder, cut in bite size pieces
- 6 ounces mozzarella cheese, grated
- 2 cups spaghetti sauce, more or less to suit taste

Shell and clean shrimp. Boil noodles. Mix ricotta cheese, eggs, onions (scallions), mushrooms, and Old Bay. Fold mix into crabmeat until chunky. Use a 9 × 12 baking dish for the following 3 layers of filling and four layers of noodles. Layer bottom of dish with noodles, and place cut up flounder pieces on top. Sprinkle one-third of the mozzarella cheese on flounder. Place another layer of noodles on top. Place scallops, half of crab mix, and one-third of mozzarella over noodles. Add some spaghetti sauce. Lay down another layer of noodles. Place shrimp, rest of crab mix, rest of mozzarella, and some more spaghetti sauce on these noodles. Cover it all with last layer of noodles and rest of the spaghetti sauce. Bake 1 to 1½ hours or until bubbly at 350 degrees.

Serves: 8-10

BOB HELSLEY is design manager for WJLA-TV.

Bob Helsley
Linguini with White Clam Sauce

- ¼ cup olive oil
- 2 scallions, chopped
- 3 cloves garlic, finely chopped or grated
- ¼ cup white wine
- 1 6½-ounce can chopped or minced clams
- 1 10-ounce bottle clam juice
- 2-3 tablespoons parsley, chopped
- ½ teaspoon oregano
- Salt and pepper to taste
- 2 tablespoons cornstarch, thinned with clam juice
- 2 servings linguini noodles, cooked according to package directions

Heat olive oil in pan on high heat. Add scallions and garlic and cook approximately 2 minutes. Be careful not to burn or brown. Add white wine, clams, bottled clam juice, parsley, oregano and salt and pepper. Cook a few minutes and thicken slightly with some cornstarch. Cook linguini according to package directions for al dente noodles. Drain.

Serve sauce over noodles.

Variation: Add some small fresh cherrystone clams to recipe and cover until clams open. This really makes it extra good.

Serves: 2

"This is a recipe which I have developed and improvised over the years. It is cheap to prepare, fast and quite tasty. I prefer it made with lots of garlic, but depending on your tolerance for garlic, you can alter it accordingly. The cornstarch is not necessary, but I found that by thickening the sauce a little, it helps cling to the pasta better."

JOE GORHAM is host of WHUR-FM's "In Flight" show.

Joe Gorham
Meat Loaf Rock 'N' Roll

- 1 pound ground beef or ground steak
  Salt and pepper
- 6-8 slices american cheese, or your favorite cheese

Season meat well with salt and pepper and your favorite spices or tenderizers. Roll meat out to make a large patty. Lay cheese slices overlapping across meat patty. Roll patty to form cheese-meat swirl inside the center. Remember to leave enough room for the end of the meat patty so that cheese will not melt outside the patty. It should look like regular meat loaf. Bake in oven 1 hour at 350 degrees. Cut, serve and ROCK 'N' ROLL . . .

Serves: 6

"Hope you enjoy! This is a good recipe for trying economic times."

DR. JACK HUNTER is director of post-production and former president of the Educational Film Center. A former program director at WETA-TV, he has worked in film and broadcasting since 1948. He is a former president of the Washington Chapter of N.A.T.A.S. and is a member of the National Awards Committee for N.A.T.A.S.

Jack Hunter
Oregon Trail Hearty Omelettes (Sunday Brunch Style)

- 2½ -3 large eggs
- 1 teaspoon water
- 1 tablespoon safflower oil
- ¼- ½ medium onion, chopped
- ⅛ cup cheddar cheese, shredded
  Parmesan or romano grated cheese
- 3 tablespoons hot salsa or taco sauce

Break eggs into a mixing bowl, add water and stir with a French whip. Set aside. Heat oil in a 10" teflon frying pan. Add the onions and cheddar cheese. Saute, stirring constantly to keep the cheese fluid. After a minute or so, add the eggs. Continue stirring as long as the mixture continues to flow. Just before it locks up, shake pan to level mix. Sprinkle parmesan or romano cheese over the face of the still-heating omelette. (This holds the heat and helps firm up the mix.) As soon as the last liquid egg has hardened, spoon the salsa in a 2-inch strip across the diameter of the omelette. Fold in both sides in thirds, across the salsa, slip onto a plate and consume with gusto while it's hot.

Serves: 1

"Most of the smarts for this concoction came, strangely enough, from a chef on a local television program who stirred around with some leftover chuck wagon tricks acquired while growing up in Cheyenne. We've tried lots of variations, but always seem to come back to this."

VARIATIONS: There's enough flavor here that the health-conscious can leave out half of the egg yolks (ah say, that cholesterol, folks!) and hardly know the difference. On the other hand, some folks just have a compulsion to use rich creamery butter instead of the oil. The good stuff in the middle can include about anything else you traditionally love in an omelette (green peppers, mushrooms, ham, etc.) and the hot sauce can be fired up with some crushed red peppers, or cooled down with a mild taco sauce to the level that tickles your palate. Whatever variation, this'll get your breath a-steamin' on a crisp mountain morning!

JOHN DOUGLASS is on the faculty of the School of Communication at American University where he heads the graduate film and video production program. He is the current president of the Washington Chapter of N.A.T.A.S. He is a parent at the Broadcasters' Child Development Center.

John Douglass
Scalloped Oysters and Mushrooms

4 dozen oysters
¾ pound mushroom caps, sliced
1½ tablespoons onion, grated
1 cup butter
1½ cups cracker crumbs
1½ cups French bread crumbs
¾ teaspoon salt
⅓ teaspoon pepper
⅓ teaspoon nutmeg
⅛ teaspoon savory
3 tablespoons cream

Drain oysters and reserve liquid. Saute mushrooms in 2 tablespoons of the butter. Add grated onions and continue to cook until mushrooms and onions are tender. Season cracker and bread crumbs with salt, pepper, nutmeg and savory. Melt ¾ cup of the butter and add to crumb mixture. Stir in cream and ¼ cup oyster liquor. Butter a 9 × 12 baking dish and put a thin layer of crumb mixture on bottom. Add a layer of oysters and a layer of mushroom mixture. Repeat layers of crumbs, oysters, mushrooms, and end with a layer of crumbs. Dot with remaining butter and bake for 30 minutes at 375 degrees.

Serves: 8

GAIL FARBER is a segment producer for WDVM's "Capital Edition."

Gayle Farber
Green Pasta with Tomato Sauce

- 6 slices bacon
- 3 cloves garlic
- 1 bunch scallions
- 6 tomatoes
- Dash basil
- Dash Italian seasoning
- Dash salt and pepper
- 1 pound spinach pasta prepared according to package directions
- Parmesan cheese

Fry bacon and set aside. In remaining bacon grease, saute garlic and chopped scallions. Chop tomatoes into bite-sized chunks and add to pan. Saute on low heat. Tomatoes will start to make own sauce. Cook only until tender, not mushy. Add seasonings to taste and add any others you like for Italian flavor. Boil pasta; do not overcook. Serve plates individually and sprinkle with crumbled bacon and parmesan cheese. You can also add vegetables to this sauce if desired—broccoli, carrots, etc.

Serves: 4

JOE RICE is an engineer with WDVM-TV.

Joseph Rice
Pepper Steak and Salad

- 1 cup uncooked rice
- 1 8-ounce steak, lean
- 1 small onion
- 1 small tomato
- 1 green pepper
- 7 large mushrooms
- ½ head lettuce
- 1 carrot
- 1 teaspoon butter
- 1 teaspoon oil
- Dash Accent, garlic powder, salt and pepper
- 1 tablespoon soy sauce
- 2 tablespoons water

Cook rice. Chop steak in bite-size pieces. Chop onion, tomato, pepper, mushrooms, and lettuce. Shred carrot. Set aside what you want for salad, reserving some onion, pepper and tomato for steak. Melt butter and oil in large frying pan at medium temperature. Place steak in pan and begin to fry. Add onion, pepper, and tomato and season as you like with Accent, pepper, garlic powder, and salt. Cook for five minutes or until steak is brown. Add soy sauce and water and stir. Now you can either add rice and stir for 1 minute, or serve over rice on your plate. Toss extra salad ingredients in bowl, add favorite dressing, and dig in!

Serves: 1-2

ANDREA ROANE joined Eyewitness News at WDVM-TV in 1981. She is currently the anchor of the noon news and a reporter. Prior to joining Channel 9, she was host and chief correspondent for WETA-TV's "Metro Week In Review." A native of New Orleans, she has worked in broadcasting since 1975.

Andrea Roane
Stuffed Bell Peppers

- 9 large bell peppers
- ¼ cup vegetable oil
- 1 onion, finely chopped
- 1 stalk celery, finely chopped
- 2-4 sprigs parsley, finely chopped
- 1 small bell pepper, finely chopped
- 6 cloves garlic, finely chopped
- 2 8-ounce cans tomato sauce
- 1½ pounds shrimp
- Salt to taste
- White pepper
- Cayenne pepper
- Bread crumbs
- 1 cup water
- 16 ounces crabmeat
- Dash of tabasco

Preheat oven to 350 degrees. Split peppers in half horizontally, and remove seeds and membranes. Set aside. Peel, devein and chop shrimp. Set aside. Heat oil in large skillet. Add onions, celery, parsley, small bell pepper, and garlic and saute 15-20 minutes or until cooked. Add ½ can tomato sauce, and shrimp. Blend together, add salt, pepper, bread crumbs and crabmeat. Place stuffing in peppers. Arrange in baking dish. Add remainder of tomato sauce and 8 ounces of water to bottom of baking dish. Spoon sauce over peppers. Cover with foil. Bake for 20-30 minutes or until peppers are tender.

Serves: 9

RENEE ANTOSH is an account executive at WTTG and a parent at the Broadcasters' Child Development Center.

Renee Antosh
Pita Calzones

- 1 cup ricotta cheese
- ½ cup mozzarella cheese
- ½ cup provolona cheese
- ½ teaspoon oregano
- 2 tablespoons parsley, chopped
- 1 teaspoon basil
- ⅓ cup dried sliced tomatoes
- ½ cup spaghetti sauce
- 3 whole-wheat pita bread rounds

Preheat oven to 375 degrees. In large bowl, combine all ingredients, mixing in sauce last. Cut the pita breads in half to form two semi-circular pockets. Fill each pita with some of the filling and stand cut-side up in a baking dish. Bake until filling is melted and bread is crisp . . . about 10 to 12 minutes.

Serves: 2-3

BRUCE MORTON is familiar to Washingtonians as a correspondent for CBS News.

Bruce Morton
Pizza

   1 package dry yeast
   1 cup lukewarm water
   3 cups flour
   1 tablespoon oil
   1 teaspoon salt
   1 large can Italian-style tomatoes
   ½ small can tomato paste
   1 tablespoon (or more) basil
   1 tablespoon (or more) oregano
 2-3 dashes tabasco sauce
   1 large Spanish onion
   1 pound spicy ground pork sausage
   1 pound mild ground pork sausage
   ½ pound mozzarella cheese
   4 ounces parmesan cheese, grated

Dough: Pour dry yeast into lukewarm water. Let the yeast sit for a few minutes to "proof"—that is, react to the water. Meanwhile, make a cone out of the flour. Poke a little hole in the top, and add oil (this softens the dough) and salt. When the yeast has proofed, add the yeasted water to the flour gradually, kneading as you go. Knead until the dough is smooth and elastic—until it bounces back a little when you jab it. Add a little more water or flour as needed. Put the dough in an oiled bowl, cover, and put it in a warm place to rise. This will take 90 minutes or so. The dough should double in volume. The dough can be kneaded in a food processor, using the plastic blade.

Tomato sauce: Pour off the liquid in the can of Italian-style tomatoes, then blend the tomatoes in a food processor or chop them up by hand. Add the tomato paste. Add generous quantities of basil and oregano. Add tabasco sauce. Let the sauce simmer for twenty minutes or so.

Toppings: Chop onion. Cook and drain sausage. Dice the mozzarella cheese.

Assembly: Roll out the dough onto one or more cookie sheets, depending on how thick or thin you want the crust. You'll need a floured surface on which to roll out the dough. Then add, in order, the tomato sauce, the onion, the sausage, the mozarella, and finally the parmesan. Bake in the lower third of the oven, at 500 degrees, until bubbly and done—about twenty minutes or so.

Serves: 4 (approx.)

BILL COSMOS is the executive producer for all local non-news programming at WJLA—TV. His mother was from the mountain area near Argos, Greece, and he tries to bring some of his love of this heritage home to Chevy Chase to share with his wife Farrell and son, Will.

Bill Cosmos
Yia-Yia's* Pizza

  10 8-inch flour tortillas
   1 cup freshly grated Minzithra cheese (available at Greek specialty store)
      or 1 cup parmesan or romano cheese
   1 cup Mazzola oil

In large frying pan, heat oil until it is just about ready to smoke. Carefully slip a flour tortilla around in the oil being careful not to splatter the oil. Use tongs to hold or remove tortilla. Let it fry for 8-10 seconds on one side. The tortilla will puff up which is o.k., unless it puffs up too much, at which time you can puncture the bubble with the tips of the tongs. After about 10 seconds turn tortilla over to allow other side to brown evenly. When that happens, lift tortilla with the tongs, holding it over the pan for a moment to allow excess oil to drip back into pan. Place browned and crisp Yia-Yia pizza on a plate. Sprinkle immediately with cheese to taste. (The more cheese the better for me.) Repeat the process until all tortillas are fried, stacked and sprinkled with cheese.

Serves: 8-10

"Before the stroke which made it impossible for Yia-Yia to mix and knead the dough for this incredibly good appetizer, she would toss some flour, salt, water and a little bacon grease into a bowl, knead it and roll out 8 inch round tortilla thin flats of it and stack it until she was ready to cook. Since her stroke, I've been forced to cheat on the process just to keep my kids from being denied a taste of their Greek heritage. The recipe above is all it takes to cheat yourself into heaven."

*Yia-Yia means grandmother in Greek.

DONNA JACKSON is a secretary in the Creative Services Department at WHMM-TV.

Donna Jackson
Poor Boy Sandwich

1 whole-wheat pita bread round
Assorted cheese slices (longhorn, swiss, colby, feta or cheddar)
Alfalfa sprouts
Cucumber slices
Mayonnaise

Heat pita bread for 1-2 minutes in 350 degree oven. Remove from oven and stuff with cheeses, alfalfa sprouts and cucumber slices. Add just a smidgen of mayonnaise. It's great!

Serves: 1

LORRAINE LEE is associate producer of WTTG's "Capital City Magazine."

Lorraine Lee
Pork Charles

- 1 pound boneless pork
- 1 clove garlic, sliced
- ¾ teaspoon ground ginger
- 3 tablespoons dry sherry
- 6 tablespoons soy sauce
- ¼ cup hoisin sauce
- 2 tablespoons cornstarch
- 3 cups shredded cabbage
- 1 medium red pepper, sliced in strips
- 1 medium green pepper, sliced in strips

Partially freeze pork; slice thinly across the grain into bite-size strips; set aside. In a bowl combine garlic clove, ground ginger, dry sherry, and 3 tablespoons soy sauce. Add the pork and allow to marinate for one hour. Preheat a large skillet or wok; add pork and marinade mixture and allow to cook 3 to 4 minutes. In a small bowl, combine hoisin sauce, 3 tablespoons soy sauce and cornstarch; mix well. Add this mixture to pork and the marinade mixture in wok or skillet and stir until thickened. Add cabbage and red and green peppers. Cook and stir for 2 minutes. Serve over hot cooked rice.

Serves: 5

BILL TRUMBULL has been with WMAL radio since 1960 and has been part of the Trumbull and Core team for more than a decade. The entertaining team is heard each afternoon during drive time. Before coming to WMAL, Bill worked in Massachusetts, did a stint with the US Army Band and worked with the Voice of America. He likes to cook and lives with his family in Darnestown.

Bill Trumbull
Pork Chops and Sour Cream

- 4 large pork chops
- Salt
- Pepper
- Sage
- Kitchen Bouquet
- Large sliced onion
- 2 cans consomme
- 3 tablespoons flour
- 1 pint sour cream

Rub pork chops with salt, pepper, sage and Kitchen Bouquet. Brown chops in small amount of fat. Drain pan. Replace chops and cover each with onion slice and two cans of consomme. Simmer, covered, for 45 minutes. Mix flour and sour cream. Remove chops and onion. Mix flour and sour cream mixture into consomme. Return chops and simmer, uncovered, for 10 minutes.

Serves: 4

"Can serve with green beans and fried apples."

JACKSON BAIN is a vice president of Gray and Company, a public relations firm. He is a former news anchor at WTTG where he also hosted "Panorama". Before joining WTTG, he worked for WRC-TV and NBC.

Jackson Bain
Indonesian Pork Kabobs

- 2 pounds lean pork
- ¼ cup peanut butter
- 3 tablespoons soy sauce
- 2 tablespoons ground coriander
- 1 tablespoon ground cumin
- ½ teaspoon chili powder
- 1 clove garlic, peeled and crushed
- 1 tablespoon lemon juice

Cut meat in 1-inch cubes. Make a paste of the peanut butter, soy sauce, spices, garlic and lemon juice in a bowl. Add cubes of meat and rub the peanut butter paste in well. Let marinate half an hour. Thread cubes of meat on skewers and broil slowly 20 to 30 minutes, six inches from the heat. Turn to brown all sides. Serve with rice and the following sauce:

- 1 cup soy sauce
- 2 tablespoons pineapple juice
- 1 clove garlic, crushed
- ¼ cup sherry
- ¼ teaspoon salt
- ½ teaspoon minced fresh gingerroot

Mix soy sauce with rest of ingredients and bring to a boil. Let cool and strain before serving. Use as a dip or pass as a sauce.

Serves: 6

FORREST SAWYER is co-anchor of "CBS Morning News."

Forrest Sawyer
Ma Sawyer's Pork Roast

- 3 or 4 pound pork loin roast
- 1 teaspoon seasoned meat tenderizer
- 1 teaspoon onion powder
- ¼ teaspoon sage
- ¼ teaspoon pepper
- ¼ teaspoon thyme
- ½ teaspoon salt
- 1 teaspoon Mrs. Dash's spice mix
- ¼ cup flour (approximate)

Select a 3 to 4 pound pork loin roast and trim excess fat. Mix next seven ingredients, adjusting amounts to suit personal taste. Rub the mixture on roast which has been dampened with water. (Dampening roast will help seasonings stick.) Prick roast with fork and wrap tightly in foil. Leave in refrigerator overnight. When ready to cook, remove foil and lightly coat roast with flour. Brown on all sides in very hot skillet. Remove from skillet and put in covered clay baking dish which has been immersed in cold water for at least 5 minutes. Add ½ cup water and drippings from skillet. Bake for 2-2½ hours at 300 degrees. Use drippings to make gravy if desired.

Serves: 4-6

"You can add fresh vegetables during the last 30-45 minutes of cooking if you like."

RICH ADAMS is editorial director for WDVM-TV where he has worked for 14 years. In addition to his current position, he has worked as assistant news director and reporter for Channel 9. He also worked for NPR, Voice of America and WCCO-TV in his native Minnesota. He is a trained emergency medical technician and active in the Bethesda Chevy Chase Rescue Squad. *(See Rich Adams' photo with his Rescue Squad Chili recipe earlier in this section.)*

Rich Adams
5 Minute Quiche for 1 Minute Managers

- 3 eggs
- 16 ounces table cream
- Tabasco sauce, to taste
- Salt to taste
- 1 cup "Fixins" (crabmeat, bacon, ham, vegetables, or whatever you want), diced, chopped or in edible form
- ½-1 cup cheddar cheese, grated
- 1 frozen deep-dish pie shell

Preheat oven to 375 degrees. Bake pie shell for 3-5 minutes. It should not be brown, just thawed and slightly baked. Remove from oven and set aside.

Mix eggs and cream in bowl and stir thoroughly. Add salt and tabasco to taste. (If making crab quiche, add Old Bay Seasoning at this point.)

Put "fixins" of choice in bottom of pie shell. Stir grated cheese in liquid mixture and pour over "fixins" in pie shell. Bake 35-40 minutes until toothpick stuck in middle of quiche comes out clean and dry. Let stand 5-10 minutes before serving.

Serves: 4-6

"Put pie shell on a cookie sheet or foil when baking. It tends to run over and mess up the oven, create smoke, set off smoke detectors, then the fire department comes—and then you have to feed 6 or 8 more people in funny boots and dirty, smelly yellow coats and red suspenders, etc. Plus the Dalmation dog, who can eat leftovers, but there probably won't be any."

TERRY MULLALLY is a videotape technician at WTTG.

Terry Mullally
Quick and Easy Quiche

   4 eggs
   1 cup sour cream
   1 cup grated cheese (cheddar, mozzarella, or provolone)
   1 can french fried onion rings
     Optional ingredients: bacon, ham, spinach, broccoli, or mushrooms

Mix and pour into prebaked pie shell or Crazy Crust (below). Bake at 400 degrees for 45 minutes.

Terry Mullally
Crazy Crust

- ½ cup all-purpose flour
- ½ teaspoon salt
- ½ teaspoon baking powder
- ¼ cup solid shortening
- ½ cup sour cream
- 1 egg

Combine all ingredients, mix until blended (about 60-70 strokes). Batter may be lumpy. Pour into greased and floured pie pan, fill and bake.

Serves: 4

HAL BRUNO is responsible for the planning and editorial content of political news at ABC television and radio networks. He hosts "Hal Bruno's Washington" on the ABC radio network. He joined ABC in 1978 after 18 years with Newsweek Magazine. He admits to being a lazy fisherman, a good skier and terrible tennis player. He is also captain of the ABC Washington Bureau softball team.

Hal Bruno
Salami and Eggs with Scallions

    Small kosher salami
4 scallions
    Oil
8 eggs
    Butter or margarine

Slice approximately 16 pieces from the salami; slice scallions. Lightly fry salami in small amount of oil, adding scallions for final minute or two of frying. Drain salami and scallions on absorbent paper. Whip and season 8 eggs for scrambling. Grease clean skillet with butter or margarine; scramble eggs, salami and scallions together.

Serve with toasted bagels and cream cheese.

Serves: 4 (For more servings, add 2 eggs, 4 salami slices, and 1 scallion for each additional portion.)

"It's great for breakfast or a light, late supper."

KATHY BYE is a parent at the Broadcasters' Child Development Center.

Kathy Bye
Sausage Ring (Breakfast)

- 2 pounds sausage
- 1½ cups cracker crumbs (saltine)
- 2 eggs
- ½ cup milk
- ¼ cup minced onion
- 1 cup chopped apple

Mix and put in mold. Bake for one hour at 350 degrees. Catch drippings.

Serves: 8

PAUL DUKE is senior correspondent for public television in Washington and moderator of "Washington Week in Review." He also hosted the PBS series, "The Lawmakers." Prior to joining PBS in 1974, he worked for NBC News, The Wall Street Journal and Associated Press.

Paul Duke
Shad Roe

    Roe of one average-sized shad
    Juice of ½ lemon
    Flour
    Salt
    White pepper
    Paprika
    Pinch of crushed thyme
    Butter
3 anchovy fillets, mashed

Simmer large roe for five minutes in water with lemon juice added. Drain, cool slightly, coat with flour seasoned with salt, white pepper, paprika, and thyme. Saute quickly in butter until both sides are lightly browned. Serve immediately with sweet butter into which several mashed anchovy fillets have been beaten.

Serves: 2

"My love for shad roe goes back to my Virginia childhood. It is best cooked simply and directly. When I now prepare it, this is the recipe guaranteed to provide a memorable meal."

FRANK NESBITT has been a filmmaker and TV producer-director-writer- and editor in public and commercial TV and in independent productions since 1967.

Frank M. Nesbitt
Spaghetti Carbonara

¼ pound bacon
1 or 2 dried red peppers
½ cup heavy cream
1 pound spaghetti (or spinach linguine)
4 tablespoons butter
Garlic powder
4 eggs
⅔ cup parmesan cheese, grated
Black pepper

Cook bacon and pour off fat. Crumble the bacon (less painful if you let it cool first). Chop up and add a dried red pepper or two. Add heavy cream. Set aside and keep warm. Put spaghetti (or spinach linguine if this meal is in color) on to boil. As they say in the old country: "Follow directions on package." While spaghetti is boiling, melt butter and add garlic powder to taste. Set aside. Beat eggs with parmesan cheese. Set aside. When the spaghetti is done, spring into action. Drain the spaghetti. Place in a hot bowl. Mix in the garlic butter using two wooden forks. Add the bacon-pepper-cream mixture. Moving carefully and quickly add the eggs and cheese, mixing carefully so the heat of the spaghetti will cook the eggs. Top with black pepper and serve immediately.

Serves: 4-6

"I am a documentary filmmaker who enjoys traveling around the country and the world for such clients as PBS, Uncle Sam and National Geographic. As I travel I collect local recipes to try when I return home to Maryland. My favorite is water. My next favorite is this pasta dish I learned from an old campesino south of Encinada. He swore his forefathers brought it over with the Conquistadors. I think he got his ethnicities scrambled by a passing Sergio Leone second unit. Either way, it's a great Spaghetti Carbonara!"

MARK DeSANTIS is promotion manager for WDVM-TV.

Mark DeSantis
Old World Spaghetti Sauce

- 1 large onion, chopped
- 2 stalks celery, chopped
- 3 cloves garlic, chopped
- 3 tablespoons olive oil (preferably extra virgin)
- 1 pork chop
- ½ pound hot Italian sausage
- 1 pound beef for stew, cut into ½ inch cubes
- 2 large cans Italian style tomatoes (you can substitute 3 pounds fresh tomatoes that have been peeled, seeded and chopped)
- 2 12-ounce cans tomato paste
- ¼ cup fresh oregano, or 2 teaspoons dried oregano
- ¼ cup fresh parsley, or 2 teaspoons dried parsley
- ½ cup freshly grated parmesan cheese (imported is better)
- Salt and pepper
- ¼ teaspoon baking soda

Saute onion, garlic and celery in the olive oil for about 5 minutes in a Dutch oven. Meanwhile, brown pork, beef and sausage in a frying pan and set aside. Add tomatoes, tomato paste, oregano, parsley, and parmesan cheese to Dutch oven. Salt and pepper to taste. Add all the meat and bring to a boil. Lower heat and simmer 2 to 3 hours or until meat is very tender. Cut sausage into slices, remove bone from pork chop and cut it up into small pieces and put back into sauce. Add baking soda and stir into sauce. Simmer 10 minutes

"Congratulations! You now have spaghetti sauce like Momma used to make. Tastes great on fresh egg or spinach pasta. This recipe can be added to 2 to 4 pounds of pasta. This sauce also freezes well. You can leave out the meat, simmer for only an hour and you've got a terrific tomato sauce by itself or with shrimp or scallops."

CYNTHIA RUDOLPH is a unit manager with WHMM-TV.

Cynthia Rudolph
Skinny Spaghetti Salad

- 1 box spaghetti
- 4 tomatoes, chopped
- 3 green peppers, chopped
- 2 onions, chopped
- Oregano, to taste (lots!)
- 3-4 leaves basil
- Oil and vinegar, to taste

Prepare spaghetti per package instructions. Drain spaghetti. Mix with tomatoes, green peppers, onions, and lots of oregano and basil. Mix spaghetti and vegetables with oil and vinegar.

Serves: 6

"It's great for a quick lunch or low-cal dinner or snack!"

CORINNE MULLEN is a parent at the Broadcasters' Child Development Center.

Corinne Mullen
Shrimp with Green Peppers

- 1 pound raw shrimp, shelled and deveined
- 6 tablespoons flour
- 2 tablespoons parmesan cheese, grated
- 1¾ teaspoon salt
- ½ cup olive oil or salad oil
- 1 clove garlic, crushed
- 6 medium green peppers, cut in strips
- Dash of black pepper

Toss shrimp with flour, cheese and 1 teaspoon of salt, coating well. Slowly heat oil in large skillet. Add shrimp and garlic, cook about 5 minutes or until

Maincourses

shrimp are golden. Remove shrimp from skillet and set aside. Add pepper strips to skillet and cook, covered, over medium heat for 10-15 minutes or until just tender, but still somewhat crisp. Return shrimp to skillet and add rest of salt, wine and black pepper to skillet. Cook, covered until heated through.

Serves: 6

"The colors are sensational. This is good served with rice."

LARRY NELSON is a parent at the Broadcasters' Child Development Center.

Larry Nelson
Shrimp Nelson

- 1 pound medium to large shrimp
- 1½ teaspoon Old Bay Seasoning
- ½ teaspoon salt
- 1 cup cider vinegar
- 1 cup water
- 1 clove garlic, minced
- ½ cup butter
- 1½ ounces Calvados
- 4 cups brown rice, cooked according to package instructions
- ½ cup celery, chopped
- ⅓ cup brine (saved from cooking shrimp)
- 5-10 cherry tomatoes, cut in half
- Lemon wedges, for garnish
- Parsley, for garnish

Boil shrimp with Old Bay, salt, vinegar and water for 15 minutes. Remove shrimp from brine, saving brine for later use. Peel and devein shrimp. Set aside.

In a separate saucepan, melt butter and saute garlic. Add shrimp and saute for 5 minutes, stirring constantly. Flame with 1½ ounces Calvados.

Cook brown rice according to package directions.

10 minutes before rice is done, add chopped celery, and ⅓ cup brine. Toss shrimp and sauce with cooked rice. Add cherry tomatoes to shrimp-rice mixture. Garnish with lemon wedges and parsley.

TV Dinners

WES SARGINSON co-anchors the 6:00 p.m. and 11:00 p.m. for WJLA-TV's News 7. Of Swedish ancestry, his recipe for Swedish meatballs has been passed down in his family for generations.

Wes Sarginson
Swedish Meatballs

- 1 pound lean ground beef
- 2 slices bread, crumbled
- 2 tablespoons onions, minced
- Salt and pepper, to taste

Sauce:
- 2 stalks celery, chopped
- 1 onion, chopped
- 1 tablespoon butter
- 1 can tomato soup, undiluted
- ½ soup can water
- 2 bay leaves
- 1 teaspoon lemon juice
- 2 teaspoons sugar

Mix ground beef, bread, 2 tablespoons onion, salt and pepper and form into balls. Set aside.

To prepare sauce, saute celery and onion in butter. Add one can tomato soup, ½ can of water, 2 bay leaves, lemon juice and brown sugar. Mix well, cooking over medium heat. Add meatballs to sauce and simmer for 45 minutes. Drain excess fat.

Serves: 4

"Best when made a day ahead and reheated before serving. Serve over rice."

DORIS McMILLON co-anchors the noon news and News 7 at 5 for WJLA. A veteran reporter, Doris recently authored a book recounting her life-long search for her natural parents.

Doris McMillon
Tortellini with Marinara Sauce

- 1 tablespoon olive oil
- 1 tablespoon sugar
- 1 clove garlic
- 1 28-ounce can Italian style tomatoes
- 8 ounce package tortellini, prepared according to package directions

Peel garlic and slice into 10-12 slices. Heat olive oil and add garlic. Do not brown garlic. Empty can of tomatoes into saucepan with garlic and olive oil. Add salt and pepper to taste. Add sugar to take bitterness out of canned tomatoes. Bring to boil for about 2 minutes, reduce heat and simmer for about 30 minutes. Prepare and drain tortellini. Pour sauce over tortellini.

Serves: 4

" 'Pasta and Cheese' sells a great tortellini in a package, and that is the kind I use. If you have extra sauce left, put it in an ice cube tray and freeze it. It always tastes better the next time out. You can defrost it in a microwave or in a little saucepan and use if over any kind of pasta."

LAWRENCE LAURENT is director on communication for the Association of Independent Television Stations and on the faculty at George Washington University. He wrote about television and other subjects for the Washington Post for more than 30 years and taught at American University for more than 20 years. He recommends this recipe first, for the frugal, and second, for the hungry. The recipe comes from Peggy Laurent's family.

Lawrence Laurent
Tuna Noodle Casserole

- 3 quarts water
- 1 tablespoon salt
- ½ pound noodles
- ⅓ cup celery, diced
- 2 tablespoons butter or margarine
- ¼ teaspoon salt
- ½ teaspoon pepper
- ½ teaspoon thyme or oregano
- 1¾ cups milk
- 2 6½-ounce cans tuna, drained
- 1 teaspoon worcestershire sauce
- 1 teaspoon lemon juice
- 1 can cream of mushroom soup
- Paprika, for garnish

Boil noodles in water to which salt has been added for 10 minutes. Drain noodles and mix thoroughly with remaining ingredients except paprika. Sprinkle paprika on top and bake for 20 to 30 minutes at 350 degrees.

Serves: 6-8

"This recipe helped bring four young Laurent children to full growth and kept father from bankruptcy and gave the family a permanent yearning for Tuna Noodle Casserole."

PAUL REECE is a reporter for WDVM-TV. He enjoys cooking in his free time.

Paul Reece
Piquant Veal

  1 piece thin-sliced veal per person, each about the size of a dollar bill. A man-sized appetite will easily handle another portion.
 12 ounce package thin ribbon noodles. I greatly prefer green (spinach) noodles in this recipe. Italian grocers stock them.
  3 large lemons
 ½ cup flour
  1 teaspoon salt
  2 teaspoons pepper
  2 tablespoons olive oil
  6 tablespoons butter
  2 tablespoons chopped parsley (fresh or freeze-dried)

This entire dish can be prepared in little more than the time required to cook the noodles, but it requires some organization in advance as the steps occur in quick succession. Some of these can be done before your guests arrive.

Pound the veal "paper" thin. (Butchers *never* pound it thin enough.) Squeeze the juice from two of the lemons, cover, save. Cut the third lemon into eighth-inch "wagonwheel" slices, save. Combine the flour, salt, pepper, save. Go enjoy your cocktail hour. Once you resume work, you're just 20 minutes from rave reviews. Bring water to boil and add noodles according to package instructions. Lay out all of the pounded veal, sprinkle with flour mixture (just a dusting), shake off excess from each piece, turn and dust other side. Put on your largest skillet to heat (an electric fry pan is excellent). Begin pre-heating a covered warming dish to eventually receive the noodles. Put olive oil, and *one* tablespoon of the butter into skillet. (If it smokes, it's too hot.) Add about one tablespoon of the lemon juice. Swirl it in, and lay in the veal. Brown well on one side (about four minutes), turn and brown the other side (about three minutes). Drain the cooked noodles. Place them in the serving dish. Layer cooked veal over the bed of noodles. Melt remaining butter in skillet. Add remaining lemon juice. Bring to a boil and remove from heat. Swirl in the parsley. Pour over veal and noodles. Garnish with lemon "wheels". Cover and keep warm.

Serves: 4-6

"This is a dish which cooks up quickly and presents a genuine gourmet flair despite its ease of preparation. One caution should be observed, however: before committing yourself to this recipe, be sure to have some form of covered warming dish to hold what is not immediately served. The thin pasta and veal will cool very quickly and the appetizing appearance and texture will be lost.

Serves well with a delicately flavored salad . . . not a vinegar dressing . . . plain breadsticks, and a crisp white wine. I recommend a good Frascati."

DIANE REHM is the host of "The Diane Rehm" Show on WAMU-FM. A native Washingtonian, her career in radio began in 1973. She loves good food, good books, tennis and softball and is an avid movie goer.

Diane Rehm
Veal Kidneys

- 2 fresh veal kidneys (beef will not do)
- 2 tablespoons butter
- 2 medium onions, sliced thin
- 12 mushrooms, fairly large, cut in quarters
- salt and pepper to taste
- 1½ cups chicken broth (either fresh or canned)
- ½ teaspoon dried thyme
- 1 bay leaf
- 3 sprigs parsley, chopped
- 2 tablespoons tawny port (use tawny port only)

Pre-heat oven to 400 degrees. Cut kidneys in half lengthwise. Then cross-cut into slices ½ inch thick. Melt butter in heavy skillet. Saute onions until translucent but not brown. Add mushrooms to skillet, and saute lightly with onions (about 5 minutes). Add sliced kidneys to skillet. Turn up flame to medium high or high so as to cook kidneys until they lose their pinkness, usually no more than five to seven minutes. Use salt and freshly ground pepper to taste. Transfer kidneys, onions, and mushrooms to ovenproof casserole. Return skillet to burner. Pour in chicken broth and heat to boiling point, while scraping bottom of skillet with wooden spoon. Add thyme, bay leaf and parsley to broth. Finally, add tawny port. Remove from flame. Pour over kidneys in casserole. Bake in preheated oven for 45 minutes. Serve over baked or steamed rice.

Serves: 4-6

GLORIA FAVA is the cook for WDVM's general manager.

Gloria Fava
Gloria's Veal Tonnato

1½ pound boneless roast of veal
1   2-ounce can anchovy filets
1   medium carrot
1   medium onion
1   stalk celery
1   clove garlic
1   bay leaf
    Salt and pepper to taste
1   3¼-ounce can tuna fish

Put the veal in a pot and cover with water. Add ½ can anchovies, carrot, onion, celery, garlic, salt, pepper and bay leaf. Boil slowly until meat is tender.

Prepare mayonnaise as follows:

2   egg yolks
1½ cups good olive oil or corn oil
¼   teaspoon dry mustard
2   teaspoons capers, chopped
1   teaspoon chopped parsley

Place 2 egg yolks in blender; add oil slowly in steady stream until thickened. Add the mustard. Divide mayonnaise in half. To one half add the can of tuna that has been mashed and the rest of the anchovies, parsley and capers.

Thinly slice the veal and put on a large platter, slice after slice. Cover with the tuna-anchovy mayonnaise and then cover with the plain mayonnaise. Decorate with sliced hard-boiled eggs or deviled eggs and sliced tomatoes. Serve cold.

Serves: 4

KATY WINN RITZENBERG is a parent at the Broadcasters' Child Development Center.

Katy Winn Ritzenberg
Vegetarian Chinese Noodles with Dan-Dan Sauce

- ½ pound Chinese noodles (or regular spaghetti)
- 3 tablespoons peanut butter or sesame paste
- 3 tablespoons sesame oil
- 3 tablespoons soy sauce
- 1 tablespoon vinegar
- 1 teaspoon chili sauce
- 1 teaspoon sugar

Boil Chinese noodles or spaghetti; drain. Heat rest of ingredients gently in saucepan. Pour hot sauce over noodles and mix.

Serves: 4-6

"Our daughter, Leah, adores tofu, and it can be cooked in many ways. One of her favorites is the above sauce over steamed (10 minutes) tofu."

Maincourses

R. RANDOLPH "Randy" RITTER is a senior videotape technician at WTTG. He shares credit for this recipe with his wife Beth. And, they both share a love of the ocean and sailing.

R. Randolph Ritter
White Conch Sauce with Linguine

- 3 or 4 slices bacon
- 3 cloves garlic, crushed
- 3 teaspoons parsley
- 1 cup ground conch
- 1 teaspoon flour
- Pinch crushed red pepper
- Pinch black pepper
- ¼ cup dry vermouth
- ¾ pound linguine cooked according to package instructions
- Grated parmesan cheese

Chop bacon in ½ inch pieces. Fry till crisp. Remove from pan to use later. Add garlic and parsley to bacon drippings, and cook about one minute until lightly browned. Add conch and cook 5 minutes. Add flour, red and black pepper and cook 3 minutes. Add vermouth. Bring to a boil. Adjust seasonings. Serve over cooked linguine with crumbled bacon and grated Parmesan cheese on top.

Serves: 4

"We use this recipe in areas where queen conch is available, and it has served us well while in the Abacos, Bahamas. The original recipe used clams."

JOHN DOUGLASS is on the faculty of the School of Communication at American University where he heads the graduate film and video production program. He is the current president of the Washington Chapter of N.A.T.A.S. and a parent at the Broadcasters' Child Development Center.

John Douglass
Zucchini and Sausage

- 2 pounds zucchini
- ½ pound sausage meat
- ¼ cup chopped onion
- ½ cup fine cracker crumbs
- 2 eggs, slightly beaten
- ½ cup grated parmesan cheese
- Pinch dried thyme
- Pinch dried rosemary
- Garlic salt
- Salt and pepper
- ½ teaspoon Accent

Wash zucchini and trim off ends, but do not peel. Cook whole in boiling salted water, 15-20 minutes, or until tender. Drain <u>thoroughly</u>, chop coarsely. Drain again! Put in collander and shake. (Important to get water out.) Cook sausage meat and onions until meat browns, stirring to break up into bits. Add chopped zucchini to sausage and onion, together with cracker crumbs, beaten eggs, Parmesan cheese (less 2 tablespoons), and spices. Mix well. Turn into 9-inch greased pie plate, sprinkle with remaining cheese. Bake at 350 degrees for about 45 minutes or until firm and delicately browned.

Serves: 4

"Instead of baking, you can freeze this in the pie plate. This makes a delicious frozen casserole to have on hand. I usually make 8-10 every summer for our freezer."

VEGETABLES & SIDE DISHES

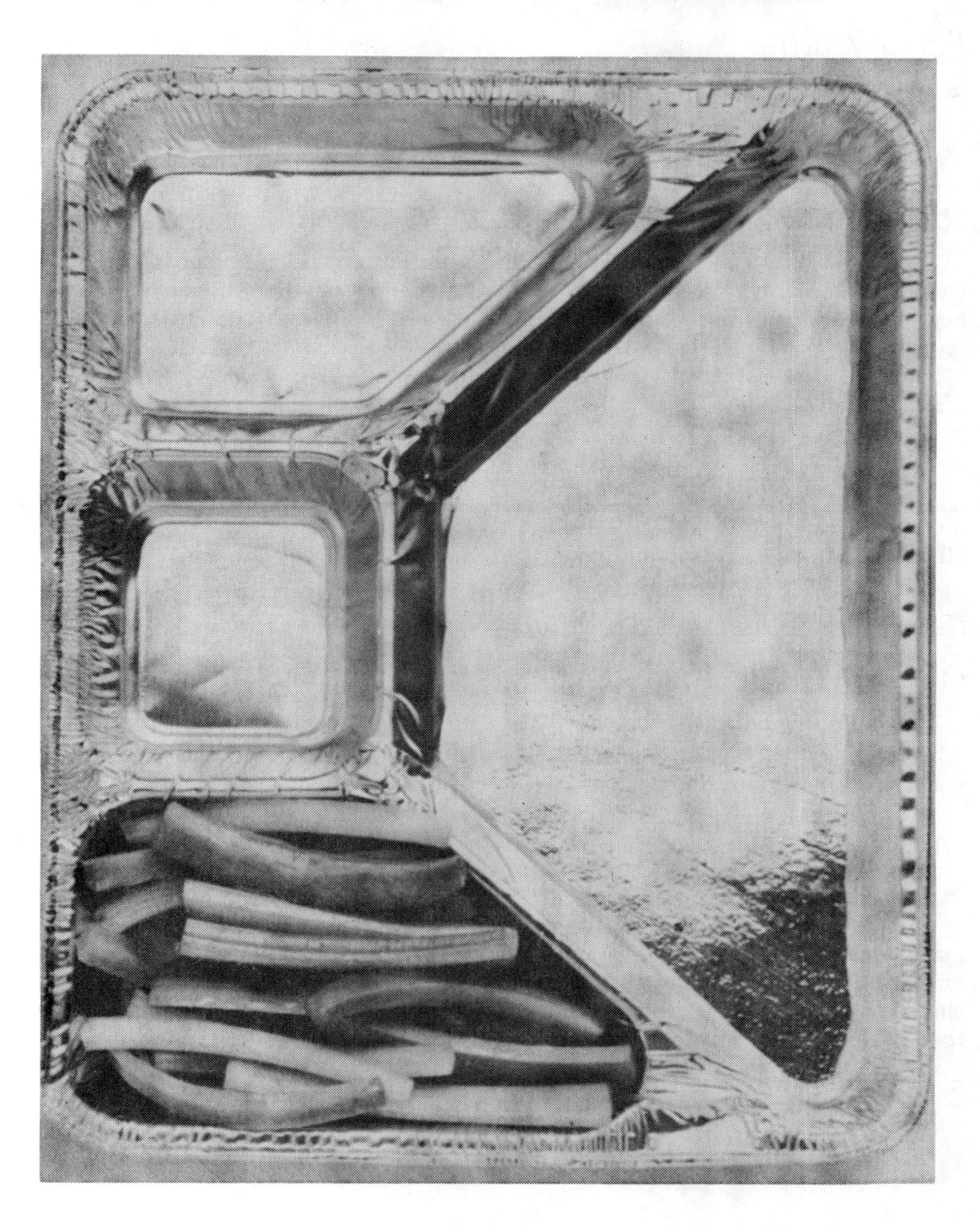

PERRY WOLFF is executive producer of "CBS Reports."

Perry Wolff
Apple Sauce

- 7-8 McIntosh apples
- 4 orange peels
- ½-¾ cups sugar
- ½ teaspoon cinnamon
- 1 pinch ginger
- ⅓ teaspoon ginger

Peel and slice apples into medium thin slices. Put apples and other ingredients into a heavy bottomed casserole and let simmer for one hour. Remove from heat, remove orange peels, and mash apples. Return to low heat and cook for approximately 15 minutes more. Cool and refrigerate.

Serves: 4

HEIDI KORZEC is a promotion writer and producer at WDCA-TV.

Heidi Korzec
Broccoli Bake

- 2 medium size bunches broccoli
- 2 cups shredded mozzarella cheese
- 1 can cream of mushroom soup
- 1 cup Bisquick
- 1 cup milk
- 2 tablespoons butter

Wash broccoli, removing leaves and tough portion of stem. Cut into managable pieces. Steam broccoli until tender. Place evenly in bottom of pan (oblong works well). Mix milk with soup and pour on top of broccoli. Sprinkle cheese on top. Mix butter with Bisquick until crumbly. Sprinkle on top of casserole. Bake at 350 for 20-25 minutes or until golden brown.

Serves: 8

Vegetables

GLENN HARRIS works in the Sports Department at WHUR-FM.

Glenn Harris
Cabbage and Carrots

- 1 medium head cabbage
- 1 green pepper, sliced in strips
- 4 carrots, cut lengthwise
- ½ cup margarine
- Vegetable salt

Melt margarine in a large skillet. Layer remaining ingredients. Repeat layers until all ingredients are used. Cook over low heat, stirring frequently until carrots are tender. Season to taste.

Serves: 4-6

SANDY PASTOOR is vice president and programming director at WTTG and a former president of the Washington Chapter of N.A.T.A.S. Before coming to Washington in 1981 she worked in the Cincinnati TV market.

Sandy Pastoor
Sweet and Sour Carrots

- 1 pound carrots, diagonally sliced
- 1 medium green pepper, seeded and cut in one inch pieces
- 1 8-ounce can pineapple packed in juice
- ⅓ cup sugar
- 1 tablespoon cornstarch
- ½ teaspoon salt
- 2 tablespoons vinegar
- 2 tablespoons soy sauce

In saucepan, cook carrots, covered, in small amount of lightly salted water until tender, 15 minutes or more. Add green pepper, cover and cook 3 more minutes. Drain and set aside.

In saucepan, combine sugar, cornstarch and salt. Stir in pineapple liquid, vinegar and soy sauce. Cook and stir until bubbly. Stir in vegetables and pineapple. Heat through.

Serves: 6

JAN BROWN MCCRACKEN is a parent at the Broadcasters' Child Development Center.

Jan Brown McCracken
Cheesy Garden Vegetables

- 2 cups cooked brown, long grain or wild rice
- 2 cups broccoli, cooked
- 2 carrots, cooked
- 1 zucchini, cooked
- 1 cup green beans, cooked
- 1 16-ounce jar marinara sauce (meatless)
- 4 ounces longhorn cheese, shredded
- 4 ounces monterey jack cheese, shredded

Put rice in bottom of baking dish. Add vegetables and cover with marinara sauce. Bake at 375 for 30 minutes. Top with shredded cheese and return to oven until cheese is melted.

Serves: 6-8

BARBARA GRUNBAUM is the government production coordinator for Montgomery Community Television.

Barbara Grunbaum
Chili Cheese Pie

- ½ cup brown rice
- 1 cup water
- 2 ounces monterey jack cheese
- ½ cup plain yogurt
- 4 ounces chopped green chilies
- Salt and pepper to taste
- 2 ounces cheddar cheese

Combine rice with water. Bring to boil. Reduce heat to simmer and cook, uncovered until all liquid is absorbed and rice is tender. Cut monterey jack cheese into strips. Cube cheddar cheese. Mix yogurt with chilis. Stir cheeses and yogurt mixture into cooked rice. Season to taste. Cover and allow cheeses to melt before serving.

Serves: 4

RENEE ANTOSH is an account executive at WTTG and a parent at the Broadcasters' Child Development Center.

Renee Antosh
Cauliflower Casserole

- 2 10½-ounce packages frozen cauliflower
- 1 can cream of chicken soup, undiluted
- ⅓ cup mayonnaise
- ½ cup cheese, grated (cheddar, longhorn, colby etc)
- Buttered cracker crumbs (optional)

Cook cauliflower according to package directions and drain. Mix all ingredients, except cracker crumbs, and place in baking dish. Cover with buttered cracker crumbs if desired. Bake for 30 minutes at 350 degrees.

Serves: 6-8

KAREN HENDERSON hosts the all night show on WMAL. Sometimes referred to as the Kate Smith of Washington, she's recognized as an outstanding vocalist and entertainer. She has sung the National Anthem at Redskins' games and has been the voice for many commercials.

Karen Henderson
Cold Vegetable Marinade

Dressing:
- 1 clove garlic
- 3 tablespoons wine vinegar
- 3 tablespoons lemon juice
- ½ cup salad oil
- 1 teaspoon salt
- ⅛ teaspoon black pepper
- 1 teaspoon Worchester sauce
- ¾ teaspoon dry mustard
- ¾ teaspoon oregano

Vegetables:
- 1 20-ounce bag frozen bean medley, thawed
- 1 16-ounce can garbanzo beans

Mash garlic. Add vinegar, lemon juice and all dry ingredients. Mix well.

Combine vegetables in large bowl and cover with marinade mixture. Marinate overnight in refrigerator.

Serves: 8

"The dressing is also great with cold asparagus or cucumbers or any favorite cold vegetables"

SUSAN STAMBERG is host of NPR's "All Things Considered" and a commentator for WDVM's "Capital Edition." She has worked in public radio for more than 20 years including several years at WAMU-FM.

Susan Stamberg
Mama Stamberg's Cranberry Relish

- 2 cups raw cranberries
- 1 small onion
- ½ cup sugar
- ¾ cup sour cream
- 2 tablespoons horseradish

Grind onion and cranberries together. Add all the other ingredients and mix. Put in a plastic container and freeze. A few hours before serving, remove the container from freezer and place in refrigerator to thaw. The relish will be thick, creamy, chunky and shocking pink.

Yield: 1½ pints

"Hope your family enjoys it. Thanks for agreeing that Mama Stamberg's Cranberry relish deserves more than 30 seconds on the radio."

LAUREN WERNER is a videotape editor for WDVM's Eyewitness News. She enjoys experimenting with new recipes whenever she's not hunting for antiques.

Lauren Werner
Williamsburg Style Green Beans

1 pound fresh green beans
5 pieces bacon
1 teaspoon rosemary

Clean, cook and drain green beans. Fry bacon, drain, saving grease and crumble. Toss beans with bacon and bacon fat. Add rosemary.

Serves: 4-6

KATY WINN RITZENBERG is a parent at the Broadcasters' Child Development Center.

Katy Winn Ritzenberg
Noodles Parmesana

½ pound noodles (rigatoni, rotini, etc.)
¾ cup parmesan cheese, grated
1 cup cottage cheese, small curd
 Garlic to taste
2 tablespoons butter
 Pepper to taste

Cook noodles according to package directions. Drain and return to pan. Mix in remaining ingredients and stir over low heat until cheese begins to melt. Amounts of cheese can be increased or decreased according to taste.

Serves: 4

"This recipe can also be served as a vegetarian main course."

Vegetables

PAT LAWSON has been with WRC since 1982. She is currently producing "Special Focus," a daily segment for "Live At Five." She co-anchored the noon news for 2½ years and worked as a general assignment reporter for WRC. She previously worked at WBAL in Baltimore and at Washington's WTOP radio.

Pat Lawson
Macaroni Casserole

1½ cups elbow macaroni, cooked according to package directions for well done
1 cup grated cheese (longhorn, cheddar and monterey jack mixed together to taste)
2 eggs
1½ cups evaporated milk
4 tablespoons butter, melted
Salt and pepper to taste
Paprika

Preheat oven to 350 degrees.

Beat together, eggs, evaporated milk, add butter, season with salt, pepper and paprika to taste. Spread a layer of macaroni in casserole dish. Pour in a little egg and milk mixture. Sprinkle layer with part of cheese. Repeat layer of noodles, milk and egg mixture, and cheese, and seasonings. Bake at 350 for 25 minutes.

Serves: 4

Note: Make sure the entire casserole is adequately soaked when it goes into oven.

GAIL FLANNIGAN is a producer and director for WJLA specials and documentaries.

Gail Flannigan
Mesquite Fever

  6 small zucchini
  6 baby eggplants
  1 pound fresh green beans
  6 new potatoes, scrubbed
  ½ cup olive oil
  2 tablespoons coarse salt
  3 medium sweet red or green peppers

Wash and dry vegetables, leave stems on and arrange in shallow baking pan large enough to hold them in one layer. Drizzle with olive oil and sprinkle with salt. Bake at 375 degrees until brown and slightly shriveled. Zucchini and eggplant will cook in approximately 30 minutes and potatoes in one hour. Remove individual vegetables as they become tender and arrange on serving platter. Serve at room temperature.

To cook on grill: Use two layers of aluminum foil with holes poked in top and bottom instead of baking dish. Set vegetables wrapped in foil on grill. Cover grill if your grill has a lid and cook as directed below.

Serves: 6

"During the summer, just about everything is cooked on a mesquite grill at my house. I've adapted a recipe from the "Silver Palate" which turns out great on the grill."

MIKE BUCHANAN joined WDVM-TV (then WTOP-TV) in 1970 and has been reporting for Eyewitness News ever since except for 3 months in 1973 when he was covering the White House for UPI-TV. Before coming to Channel 9 he was a reporter and news director for WTTG. He has also worked in Chicago and Oklahoma.

Mike Buchanan
Noodles' Buckaroo

- 8 ounces bourbon
- 1 ounce club soda
- ½ pound butter
- 2 tablespoons garlic
- 1 pound noodles, cooked according to package directions
- 1 tablespoon fresh ground pepper
- 1 teaspoon salt

Mix 8 ounces bourbon with club soda. Add three ice cubes and drink it.

Then mix garlic, butter cooked noodles, salt and pepper with any additional ingredients of your choice. It will taste delicious.

FRED WEISS uses his skills as a meteorologist during daily weather forecasts on WJLA-TV's "Morning Report" and News 7 at Noon. He is also Channel 7's staff announcer.

Fred Weiss
German Potato Salad

- 14 small red potatoes
- 3 slices bacon
- ¾ cup cold water
- 2 tablespoons flour
- 2 tablespoons sugar
- 1 teaspoon salt
- ½ teaspoon pepper
- ¼ cup white vinegar
- 1 tablespoon onion, finely chopped
- Minced parsley or chives for garnish

Wash, boil and cool potatoes. Cut into thin slices. Cube slices of bacon. Fry in large skillet until crisp. Remove from pan, and set aside to drain, leaving grease in pan. To ¾ cup cold water, add flour, sugar, salt, pepper and vinegar. Mix until smooth. Add this mixture to the grease in the pan along with onion. Cook slowly, stirring frequently until thickened to the consistency of gravy and turning somewhat glossy. Add potatoes and heat through, mixing with wooden spoon to keep slices from breaking. Garnish with bacon bits. Add parsley or chives, if desired. Serve hot.

Serves: 4-6

DIMETRIUS JACKSON is an operations technician with WHMM-TV. He has also worked as a videotape editor with NBC and WJLA-TV.

Dimetrius Jackson
Uncle Jack's Fresh Cut, Skin-On Home-Did French Fries

6- 10 medium to large potatoes
Vegetable oil (enough to cover potatoes in skillet — amount will vary according to size of pan)

Choose large potatoes and soak them in cold water for a few minutes. Scrub each with a vegetable brush to remove dirt from skin. Inspect each potato and remove all eyes, buds and funny looking skin with the point of a knife. Cut potato in half lengthwise, then cut each half in three or four slices depending on thickness.

Make your next cut right angles to the previous cuts to make the french fry strips. As you cut the fries, inspect them again and remove any bad spots. Put in collander to dry.

Heat oil in pan. Use enough oil to cover fries and check for oil's readiness by placing a "test tater" in pan. When the fry floats . . . little bubbles and all . . . the oil is ready.

Fill pan with fries and cook for approximately 10 minutes over high heat or until they just start getting golden. Do not pack too tightly in pan and keep covered with oil. Remove from heat and drain on paper towels.

Serves: 8

"Long potatoes make prettier fries. Do yourself a favor and try these things without salt or catsup"

MIKE LEWIS is the voice of Channel 9. As staff announcer for WDVM-TV, you hear his voice on news show opens, station promos and i.d.'s He also has a wide range of national credits as writer producer and talent on radio and TV spots. He admits that his wife Susan, didn't marry him for his cooking. *(See Mike's photo in the maincourse section with his recipe for Chicken Breasts with Sesame Seeds.)*

Mike Lewis
New Potatoes In Cumin Vinaigrette

- 1 pound tiny new potatoes
- 2 tablespoons olive oil
- ¼ teaspoon ground cumin
- 2 tablespoons red wine vinegar
- 1 clove garlic
- Freshly ground black pepper, to taste

Scrub potatoes and cook in boiling water until tender, about 20 minutes.

Beat oil with cumin and vinegar in serving bowl. Press garlic clove through press into dressing. Mix with pepper.

When potatoes are ready, drain and cut in half or quarters directly into serving bowl in which dressing was mixed. Stir with dressing to coat well.

Serves: 4-6

Mike Lewis
Butternut Squash With Anise

- 1 pound butternut squash
- 1 teaspoon anise seed
- 1 tablespoon unsalted butter

Peel squash. Dice or slice and cook in boiling water until soft, about 7-10 minutes. Drain. Place in food processor with anise seed and butter and puree.

Serves: 3

PAM SIMON is Director of Broadcasters' Child Development Center.

Pam Simon
Hash Brown Potato Casserole

- 1 2 pound bag frozen hash brown potatoes
- 1 can cream of celery soup
- 1 can cream of potato soup
- 1 can cheddar cheese soup
- 1 cup sour cream
- ½ cup grated cheddar cheese

Mix all ingredients, except grated cheese. Do not thaw potatoes. Put in 9" × 13" or 3 quart casserole dish. Bake at 350 degrees for 20 minutes. Remove from oven and top with grated cheese. Return to oven and bake 20 minutes more or until bubbly.

Serves: 12-16 If you want to serve a smaller number, freeze portion of <u>unbaked mixture</u> for another time.

"This dish is excellent with baked ham."

Pam Simon
Rice Pilaf Casserole

- 1 8-ounce package Uncle Ben's Long Grain and Wild Rice
- 1 can cream of mushroom soup
- ½ cup raisins (golden raisins taste best)
- 2 tablespoons slivered or chopped almonds
- 1 3 or 4-ounce can sliced mushrooms, drained
- ½ cup celery, chopped

Cook rice according to package directions. Add rest of ingredients to mix. Put in 2 quart casserole dish. Bake uncovered at 350 degrees for 30 minutes.

Serves: 6-8

DONNA JACKSON is a secretary in the Creative Services Department at WHMM-TV.

Donna Jackson
Louisiana Rice Dressing (Dirty Rice)

- 3 sets chicken giblets, ground
- 2 large onions, ground
- 1 cup ground celery
- 6 tablespoons butter
- 2 dozen oysters, ground
- ¼ cup oyster liquid
- ½ cup minced parsley
- 2 cloves garlic, minced
- ½ cup ground green onions
  Salt, pepper and cayenne (to taste)
- 4 cups cooked rice

Saute giblets, onions and celery in butter until onions and celery are soft and giblets are brown. Add remaining ingredients except seasonings and rice. Stir, cover and simmer 10 minutes. Add seasonings, stir in cooked rice and heat thoroughly. Yields enough stuffing for a 10-pound turkey or may be baked in greased casserole dish in 350 degree F. oven 20 minutes.

Serves: 8-10 (approx.)

Note: The real secret is that the oysters, giblets and vegetables are <u>ground</u>, not chopped.

FRAN MURPHY is executive producer of WTTG's "PM Magazine." Prior to joining WTTG in 1983, Fran worked in Milwaukee.

Fran Murphy
Ratatouille

- 1 small eggplant (apx. 1 pound)
- 2 medium zucchini
- 2 small green peppers
- 4 ripe tomatoes or 1 20-ounce can Italian-style tomatoes
- 1 large onion
- 1 clove garlic
- ½ teaspoon sugar
- Salt and pepper to taste
- ⅓ cup olive oil

Peel eggplant and cut in strips ½ inch thick by 2½ inches long. Cut zucchini in bite size pieces. Put zucchini and eggplant in large bowl. Sprinkle with heaping teaspoon salt and cover with plate weighted down with unopened canned goods. Let stand for 30 minutes to remove excess moisture. Drain and pat dry. Clean and seed green peppers and slice in thin strips. Repeat with onion and garlic. Peel fresh tomatoes and slice in wedges, remove most seeds. If using canned tomatoes, drain thoroughly.

Preheat oven to 325 degrees. In large pan, heat 3 teaspoons olive oil, saute onion and garlic until lightly brown. In a 2 quart oven-proof casserole layer the vegetables in the following order: spoonful of onion, ⅓ of tomato wedges, ½ green peppers, ½ eggplant and zucchini mixture. Sprinkle each layer with sugar, and salt and pepper. Repeat layers ending with onions and remaining tomatoes. Pour remaining oil over top and cover. Bake for one hour.

Serves: 4-6

"Make a day ahead. Good hot or cold."

KATE ATKINS is a pre-school teacher at the Broadcasters' Child Development Center

Kate Atkins
Zucchini-Tomato Casserole

- 2 cups sliced zucchini
- 1 cup onion, thinly sliced
- 2 small tomatoes, sliced
- ⅓ cup fine bread crumbs
- Salt
- Pepper
- 1 tomato, cut in wedges
- ½ cup grated cheese

Layer half of the zucchini, onion, tomatoes, and bread crumbs. Sprinkle with salt and pepper to taste. Repeat layers. Top with tomato wedges. Cover and bake at 375 for 1 hour. Uncover and sprinkle with cheese. Return to oven until cheese melts.

LAUREN WERNER is a videotape editor for WDVM's Eyewitness News. She enjoys experimenting with new recipes whenever she's not hunting for antiques.

Lauren Werner
Sweet Potato Casserole

- ¼ cup granulated sugar
- ½ cup brown sugar, packed
- ½ cup orange juice
- ⅓ cup melted butter
- 2 1 pound 5 ounce cans vacuum packed sweet potatoes
- 1 teaspoon salt
- 1 teaspoon cinnamon
- ⅔ cup pecan halves

Syrup: Combine granulated sugar, 2 tablespoons orange juice, and 2 tablespoons melted butter. Set aside.

Mash sweet potatoes until smooth. Whip eggs, add remaining brown sugar, orange juice and butter plus one teaspoon salt and one teaspoon cinnamon. Mix together and add to potatoes. Spread evenly in a casserole dish and top with pecan halves. Pour syrup over top and bake at 375 degrees for 40 minutes.

Serves: 6-8

"This dish is not too sweet."

BOB LEVEY is a columnist for The Washington Post and a commentator for WJLA-TV and WETA-FM. During his 18 years at the Post, he has covered politics, sports, the courts and features. He has been a columnist for 4 years. He is a champion tournament bridge player.

Bob Levey
Snow Peas and Peppers

1 pound fresh snow peas, washed and trimmed
2 sweet red peppers, cored and sliced in ¼ inch strips
1 large yellow onion
2 cloves garlic
2 tablespoons vegetable oil
4 tablespoons water
   Salt to taste

In a large skillet, combine oil, onions and garlic pressed through garlic press. Saute over lowest possible heat until onions are translucent. Increase heat to medium and add peppers until peppers begin to soften, approximately 5 minutes. Set aside until right before serving. Just before you are ready to serve, return to high heat until sizzling, and add snow peas and water. Stir and cover tightly, cooking for three minutes or until snow peas turn bright green. Remove from heat and serve immediately. Add salt to taste. Snow peas should be crunchy while peppers should be slightly soft.

Serves: 4-6

"This colorful dish complements simply prepared entrees such as broiled fish or chicken.

DESSERTS

MARGE KUMAKI is a news reporter and anchor for WMAL radio. She is also a parent at the Broadcasters' Child Development Center.

Marge Kumaki
Easy Moist Banana Nut Cake

- 3 cups flour
- 2 cups sugar
- 1 teaspoon cinnamon
- 1 teaspoon salt
- 1 teaspoon baking soda
- 1 teaspoon vanilla
- 1½ cups vegetable oil
- 3 ripe bananas
- 3 eggs
- 6 ounces crushed pineapple with juice
- ½ -1 cup walnuts or pecans, use amount to suit taste

Frosting
- 6 ounces cream
- ½ cup butter, softened
- 1 teaspoon vanilla
- Confectioners sugar, to suit taste

Preheat oven to 300 degrees. Grease and flour bundt pan.

Mix by hand, do not use electric mixer to combine ingredients. Mix all ingredients for cake together until well blended. Put in bundt pan and bake for 1½ hours or until toothpick comes out clean when inserted in cake. Cool cake in pan for 1 hour before removing.

To make frosting combine all ingredients except sugar. Add sugar slowly until desired consistency is reached.

Serves: 8-10

MARLENE SHIPPY-KOEBBE is an administrative assistant for Montgomery Community Television.

Marlene Shippy-Koebbe
Banana Pudding Supreme

- 1 package banana or vanilla pudding mix, prepared according to package directions
- 3 bananas
- 1 box vanilla wafers
- 2 egg whites

Prepare pudding according to package instructions. Let cool. Slice bananas into slices that are not too thin. Beat egg whites until stiff. In a 2 quart casserole or ovenproof dish, layer vanilla wafers, bananas and pudding ending with a layer of vanilla wafers. Top entire mixture with beaten egg whites. Form egg whites into peaks. Broil until light brown.

Serve warm or cold.

Serves: 4-6

BOB KANNER is a videotape editor for CBS News. Before joining CBS, he worked at WTTG for several years. While Bob enjoys eating the Blackbottom Miniatures, he gives credit to his wife Michele for making them.

Bob Kanner
Blackbottom Miniature

Light Batter:
- 8 ounces cream cheese
- 1 egg
- ⅓ cup sugar
- ⅛ teaspoon salt
- 8 ounces chocolate chips

Dark Batter:
- 1½ cups flour
- ¼ cup cocoa
- 1 teaspoon vanilla
- 1 teaspoon salt
- 1 cup water
- 1 cup sugar
- 1 teaspoon baking soda
- ⅓ cup vegetable oil
- 1 tablespoon white vinegar

To make light batter: Beat cream cheese and add egg, sugar and salt. Mix well. Add chocolate chips. Set aside.

To make dark batter: Blend all ingredients together and mix well.

Line minature baking tins with minature cupcake papers, then fill with:
- 1 tablespoon dark batter on bottom
- 1 teaspoon light batter on top.

Do not mix the batters together, just lay the light batter on top of the dark in the tins. Bake for 15-20 minutes at 350 degrees.

Yields: 48

FRANCES STACHOW SEEGER is a producer at WJLA-TV. She was program acquisition manager for Montgomery Community TV. She worked at WTTG for several years and was producer of Channel 5's "Panorama." She is a parent at the Broadcasters' Child Development Center.

Frances Stachow Seeger
Peanut Butter Pie

- 1 cup sugar
- 1 cup dark Karo syrup
- 3 eggs
- ½ cup peanut butter (smooth or chunky)
- 1 teaspoon vanilla extract

Mix all ingredients and pour into an unbaked 9" pie shell. Bake for 10 minutes at 350°, then reduce to 325° and bake for 40 minutes more. Serve room temperature.

Frances Stachow Seeger
Fudge Pie

- 1 stick oleo
- 2 squares bitter chocolate (Baker's)
- 1 cup sugar
- 2 eggs
- ¼ cup flour
- ½ teaspoon salt
- 1 teaspoon vanilla

Melt chocolate over low heat. Remove from heat and add sugar, then 2 eggs, slightly beaten. Add flour, salt and vanilla. Pour into 7" or 8" (small) greased pie pan. Bake 20 minutes at 350°. Serve slightly warm or at room temperature.

STEVE BELL is ABC's anchorman on "World News This Morning" and news anchor for "Good Morning America." A native of Iowa, Steve joined ABC News in 1967 as a correspondent based in New York. He gives credit for this recipe to his wife, Joyce.

Steve Bell
Brownies

- ½ cup margarine
- 1 cup sugar
- 2 eggs
- ½ teaspoon salt
- ¾ cup flour
- ¼ cup cocoa

Frosting:
- 2 tablespoons margarine
- ½ box confectioners sugar
- 1-2 tablespoons evaporated milk (approximate)
- Cocoa, to taste

Cream together sugar and margarine. Add eggs, salt, flour and ¼ cup cocoa. Mix all ingredients until well blended. Pour into well greased square baking dish. Bake for 20 minutes at 350 degrees. Remove from oven and cool.

To make frosting: Mix margarine and confectioners sugar until well blended, adding just enough evaporated milk to make a smooth icing consistency. Add cocoa a little (one teaspoon) at a time, until desired chocolate flavor is obtained. Whip entire mixture until smooth.

Spread evenly over brownies and cut in squares.

Yield: 12

YOLANDA GASKINS joined WTTG in 1985 as co-host of "PM Magazine."

Yolanda Gaskins
Brownie Alaska

- 1½ cups strawberry ice cream
- 2 cups pistachio ice cream
- 3 cups vanilla ice cream
- 1 baked 8 inch square fudgy brownie layer cooled
- 3 egg whites
- ¼ teaspoon salt
- ¼ teaspoon cream of tartar
- 6 tablespoons sugar

Sauce:
- 4 ounces Baker's German sweet chocolate
- 1⅓ cups evaporated milk
- 1 cup miniature marshmallows

To make sauce: Place chocolate, evaporated milk and marshmallows in saucepan. Stir constantly over very low heat until mixture is smooth. Can be kept warm or reheated in top of double boiler.

After you've made sauce, prepare the following: Soften each flavor of ice cream just before using. Press strawberry ice cream into 1½ quart mixing bowl. Freeze until firm. Repeat with pistachio and vanilla ice creams. Unmold ice cream from mixing bowl onto brownie layer; return to freezer while preparing meringue.

Beat egg whites with salt and cream of tartar until foamy throughout. Gradually add sugar, 1 tablespoon at a time, and continue beating until meringue forms stiff peaks. Place ice cream topped brownie layer on a brown paper lined baking sheet. Spread meringue over entire surface, sealing bottom completely. Bake for 5-6 minutes at 450 degrees or until meringue is golden brown. Transfer to serving platter and serve at once with sauce.

If dessert is made ahead, cover and store in freezer. Remove from freezer 20 minutes before serving for ease in slicing.

Serves: 10

VINNY BROWN is heard on weekends on Q107.

Vinny Brown
Vinny's Brownies

- 4 ounces unsweetened chocolate
- ⅔ cup shortening
- 2 cups sugar
- 4 eggs
- 1 teaspoon vanilla
- 1¼ cups all-purpose flour
- 1 teaspoon baking powder
- 1 teaspoon salt
- 1 cup pecans or walnuts, chopped

Preheat oven to 350 degrees.
Grease 13 × 9 × 2 baking pan.
Melt chocolate and shortening in large saucepan over low heat. Remove from heat. Mix in sugar, eggs and vanilla. Stir in remaining ingredients. Spread evenly in greased 13 × 9 × 2 inch baking pan. Bake for 30 minutes or until brownies start to pull away from sides of pan. Be careful not to overbake. Allow to cool. Cut in squares.

"Hope you enjoy these. Or . . . get yourself a box of Duncan Hines Brownie Mix . . . and go for it!!!! They're pretty good, too."

ROBIN CHAPMAN is co-anchor of WJLA's "Weekend Report" and a featured reporter on Channel 7's news at 11 p.m. Robin loves to cook.

Robin Chapman
Oregon Carrot Cake

- 2 cups sugar
- 2 cups flour
- 2 teaspoons baking soda
- 1 teaspoon salt
- 2 teaspoons cinnamon
- 1 cup vegetable oil
- 4 eggs
- 3 cups carrots, grated

Icing:
- 8 ounces cream cheese
- ½ cup butter
- 1 16-ounce package confectioners sugar
- 1 cup chopped nuts
- 1 teaspoon vanilla

Sift and mix dry ingredients. Combine oil and eggs. Add wet ingredients to dry, beating well. Add carrots. Pour into 2 10 inch cake pans and bake for 35 minutes at 350 degrees. Cake is very moist. Let cool before icing.

To prepare icing: Beat all ingredients together except nuts. Add nuts, stir to combine and spread on cooled cake.

Serves: 8-10

"I entered this recipe in the Gourmet Gala a few years ago and won 1st prize with it."

TERRY DRUMMOND is an associate producer with WHMM-TV.

Tammy Drummond
Absolutely Delicious Cheesecake

- 1 cup sugar
- 1 tablespoon vanilla
- 8 ounces cream cheese
- 1 cup sour cream
- 8 ounces Cool Whip
- 2 graham pie crusts
- 2 cans cherry pie filling

Mix sugar, vanilla, and cream cheese together. Stir in sour cream, then mix it slowly in blender. Add the cool whip. Spread the cheese mix evenly in graham pie crusts, then spread pie filling on top. Chill approximately 2 hours before serving.

PAUL BERRY is co-anchor of WJLA-TV's news at 5 p.m. With over a decade of service at Channel 7, he is well known to Washington viewers for his reporting and community service features such as "Crimesolvers" and "Seven On Your Side."

Paul Berry
Moist Chocolate Cake

- ½ cup margarine or butter
- 2 cups sugar
- 2 cups flour, sifted
- 2 eggs
- 1 tablespoon vanilla
- ½ cup buttermilk or sour milk
- 2 ounces unsweetened chocolate
- 1 cup hot water
- 1 teaspoon baking soda

Butter Icing
- ½ cup butter
- 8 ounces cream cheese
- 1 16-ounce package confectioners sugar
- 2 teaspoons vanilla

Melt chocolate. Cream butter and sugar. Add eggs, blend well. Sift flour and add alternately with milk. Then add ½ cup hot water to the melted chocolate. Put the other ½ cup water in a pan and bring to boil (this is important!). To this, add baking soda and immediately add this to chocolate mixture. Pour this mixture into the batter, add vanilla. Mix well. Bake in greased bundt pan for 1 hour at 350 degrees. Cake will pull away from sides of pan when done.

To prepare icing: Let cream cheese and butter soften. Beat together well. Add vanilla. Add sugar gradually and beat until smooth. Spread on cooled cake.

Serves: 8-10

MIN ROSENBERG is a former employee of WJLA-TV.

Min Rosenberg
Min's Chocolate Delights

- 1 12-ounce package chocolate chips
- 1 15-ounce can sweetened condensed milk
- ¼ cup butter (no substitutes!)
- 1 teaspoon vanilla
- 1 cup flour
- 1 cup chopped nuts

Melt butter, chips, and milk in top of double boiler. Mix in rest of ingredients and blend well. Drop by tablespoon onto greased cookie sheet. Bake for 10 minutes at 350 degrees. Watch carefully so they don't overcook. They will be soft when finished. Let sit in pan for 5-10 minutes before removing from pan. Cool 15 minutes.

Yields: Approximately 3 dozen

JOHN DOUGLASS is on the faculty of the School of Communication at The American University where he heads the graduate film and video production program. He is the current president of the Washington Chapter of N.A.T.A.S. and a parent at the Broadcasters' Child Development Center.

John Douglass
Chocolate Mousse

- ¾ cups milk, hot enough to melt chocolate
- Dash salt
- 6 ounce package chocolate bits
- 1 egg
- 1 tablespoon sugar
- 1 tablespoon instant coffee
- 1 plus capfulls rum (cocniac, bourbon, rye, brandy)

Pour all ingredients into blender and blend until smooth. Chill for one hour.

Serves: 4

"When I first got this recipe I misread my handwriting and added 1 cup of rum instead of 1 cap. It was an astounding error. The Mousse was like solid liquor. We called it "Charlotte Mousse" and have always made it that way since (with about ½ cup rum). If you try it, remember to only serve about ¼ cup per person. It's potent."

LEA THOMPSON is co-anchor of WRC-TV's "Live at 5 P.M." She also works as a consumer and investigative reporter for Channel 4 since 1973. A native of Wisconsin, she joined the station in 1970 as administrator of Editorial Services.

Lea Thompson
Lea's Lucious Chocolate Pie

- 1   8 inch pie pastry, baked
- 1   cup butter
- 1½ cups sugar
- 2   ounces semi-sweet chocolate, melted and cooled
- 2   teaspoons vanilla
- 4   eggs
- 8   ounces whipping cream, whipped and chilled
-     Shaved or curled chocolate, for garnish

Make your favorite 8 inch pie pastry, fold edge to form standing rim, flute pie crust with fork.

Bake in hot oven at 450 degrees for 10-12 minutes. Cool.

Cream butter, gradually add 1½ cups sugar, cream thoroughly. Blend in chocolate and vanilla. Add eggs, 2 at a time, beating 5 minutes after each addition with electric mixer on medium speed. Pour into cool baked pie shell. Chill several hours before serving. Immediately before serving, top with whipped cream and curled or shaved chocolate.

Serves: 4-6

"A Thompson family tradition."

JOEL LOY is co-host of WTTG's. "PM Magazine." Before coming to Channel 5, he worked in Rochester, New York. (*See Joel's photo in the Maincourse Section with his recipe for Polenta.*)

Joel Loy
Chocolate Pecan Pie

- 3 ounces unsweetened chocolate
- 3 tablespoons butter
- ¾ cup sugar
- 1 cup light corn syrup
- 3 eggs, lightly beaten
- 1 teaspoon vanilla
- 1 cup pecans, broken
- 1 9 inch pie shell, unbaked
- 8 ounces whipping cream

Preheat oven to 350 degrees.

In a saucepan, combine chocolate, butter, sugar and corn syrup and bring to boil. Add 1 tablespoon of hot mixture to eggs, stirring slowly while adding mixture. Repeat until all mixture has been added to eggs. Stir in vanilla and pecans. Pour into pie shell. Bake pie for 45 minutes or until set. While pie is baking, whip cream until it forms peaks. Chill cream in refrigerator until ready to serve. When pie is baked, remove from oven and let cool. Serve at room temperature topped with whipped cream.

SUE ANN STAAKE is a freelance producer and director. She is currently teaching at American University's School of Communication. She has worked for ABC News in Washington, and as a producer/director at WTTG and at WDVM-TV.

Sue Ann Staake
Gram King's Date Sticks

- 1 cup granulated sugar
- 1 cup walnuts, chopped
- 1 cup dates, chopped
- ¾ cups flour
- ¼ teaspoon baking powder
- 2 eggs, beaten
- Confectioners sugar, for dusting

Mix together dry ingredients except confectioners sugar like pie dough. Add eggs. Mix well. Grease and flour 9 × 9 inch pan. Bake for 45 minutes at 350 degrees. Cool slightly, cut in bars while still warm and roll in confectioners sugar.

Yields: 2-3 dozen

"This is easy to make and is one of our family's favorites."

ANDY OCKERSHAUSEN was general manager at WMAL radio.

Andy Ockershausen
Double Diabolo Cake

½ cup raisins
½ cup scotch
14 ounces semi-sweet chocolate
1 cup unsalted butter
6 eggs, separated
1⅓ cups sugar
9 tablespoons flour
1⅓ cups almonds, ground
Pinch of salt

Frosting:
8 ounces semi sweet chocolate
1 cup heavy cream

Soak raisins in scotch overnight.

Preheat oven to 350 degrees. Butter and flour a 12" cake pan. Melt chocolate in saucepan over water. Add butter bit by bit until smooth. Cool.

Separate eggs. Beat egg whites until firm and set aside. Beat egg yolks into sugar and blend until creamy. Add egg yolks and sugar mixture to chocolate. Add flour, salt and almonds. Add raisins and scotch. Fold in egg whites <u>carefully</u>. Pour into cake pan and bake for 20 minutes. Cake will be moist in middle. Let stand in pan for about 10 minutes before removing to rack to cool. To make frosting: Melt chocolate in heavy cream over medium heat, stirring constantly. Cool and frost cake. Garnish with slivered almonds, if desired.

Serves: 12

"Cake is best if made one day prior to serving."

J. C. HAYWARD is known to Washingtonians as a news anchor at WDVM-TV. She has been at Channel 9 since the early 70's, and includes work as a reporter and talk show host among her credits. J. C. assures us that none will be disappointed with this fruitless fruit pie.

J. C. Hayward
J. C.'s Fruit Pie

- 2 cups sugar
- 4 eggs
- 1 cup butter or margarine
- 2 tablespoons vinegar
- 1 cup coconut
- 1 cup walnuts, chopped fine
- 1 deep dish pie shell, unbaked
- 8 ounces whipping cream

Melt butter or margarine and cool. Add other ingredients and mix well. Pour into deep dish pie shell. Bake for 1 hour at 375 degrees. While pie is baking, whip cream until it forms peaks. Chill cream. Top pie with a thick layer of whipped cream before serving.

Serves: 8-10

"This is very rich, so slice very thin. It is similar to pecan pie, but better!"

CORINNE MULLEN is a parent at the Broadcasters' Child Development Center.

Corinne Mullen
Flan Aux Fruits

- 2 pears
- 2 apples
- ⅔ cup flour
- ½ cup sugar
- 3 eggs, slightly beaten
- 10 tablespoons butter, melted and cooled
- 1½ teaspoon baking powder
- 2 tablespoons brandy
- Pinch of salt

Mix sugar and butter. Add the eggs, flour, baking powder, salt and brandy. Mix until smooth. Peel the apples and pears. Slice into thin slices, removing all seeds. Add to dough. Pour the mixture into a greased porcelain quiche pan. Bake for 20 minutes at 350 degrees. Can be served hot, cold, or at room temperature.

Serves: 8

"I think this tastes best served at room temperature. If you don't have a porcelain quiche pan, you can substitute a 9 inch pie plate."

FAYE DAVENPORT is an associate director at ABC News and a former director at WJLA on weekends. She lives in Silver Spring with her little dog, Prince. She loves to cook, but hates to wash the dishes.

Faye Davenport
Fruit Something

- 1 cup flour
- 1 cup sugar
- 1 cup milk
- 1 teaspoon baking powder
- ½ cup butter (margarine, if you must)
- 1 quart fruit of your choice
- Sugar to sweeten fruit, if desired

Melt butter in 2 quart casserole dish. Make a batter of flour, 1 cup sugar, baking powder and milk. Heat the fruit slightly, adding sugar to taste, if desired.

Pour batter into melted butter in casserole.

Pour fruit into batter. Bake for approximately 35 minutes at 375 degrees. Serve warm with ice cream for total ecstasy.

Serves: 4-6

"I stole this recipe from one of the 75 cookbooks living in my kitchen. I like it because it is easy and sinfully yummy."

ISAAC MINTER is special projects manager at WHMM-TV.

Isaac Minter
Fast Fixin' Microwave Fudge

- 2 16-ounce packages confectioners sugar
- 1 cup unsweetened cocoa
- ½ cup milk
- 1 cup butter or margarine
- 1½ cups chopped nuts
- 2 tablespoons vanilla

In a large bowl, mix sugar and cocoa. Add milk and butter. Do not stir. Heat 4½ to 6 minutes on high heat until butter is melted. Add nuts and vanilla, stirring until smooth. Spread into well greased square baking dish. Chill until firm. Cut in squares.

Yields: 3 pounds

"For 1½ pounds of delicious fudge, halve all ingredients and cook for 2-3 minutes."

CHUCK KAVENAUGH is an artist at WDVM-TV.

Chuck Kavenaugh
Fudge

- 3 ounces Baker's bitter chocolate
- ½ cup milk
- 2 cups sugar
- ¼ cup butter
- Dash of salt
- 1 teaspoon vanilla
- 1 cup walnut pieces

Before starting, grease a square baking dish and set aside.

Combine chocolate, sugar, milk and butter in a saucepan and cook slowly until it boils. Add dash of salt while cooking. Cook, stirring constantly until mixture forms a ball when dropped in cold water. Add vanilla and mix well. Remove from heat and set pot in cold water deep enough for water to come half-way up side of outside of pan. Beat fudge rapidly until thick, but not sugary. Add nuts quickly and stir. Pour quickly into prepared baking dish.

Cool completely and cut in squares.

<u>Yields: approximately 24 pieces</u>

"How many it serves depends on the size chunks you cut. My dog once lapped a whole pan by himself. Actually, this is an old Boston recipe which I got from my grandmother."

RUTH POLLAK is a producer and writer and vice president for script development at the Educational Film Center.

Ruth Pollak
Hot Fudge Sauce Nostalgiana

  3 ounces unsweetened chocolate
2⅔ tablespoons (⅓ stick) butter
  8- 12 ounces evaporated milk
  2 cups sugar
1½ teaspoon vanilla

In a double boiler, melt the chocolate and butter. Very slowly, stir in evaporated milk a little at a time. Add the sugar. Cook over low heat for approximately 30 minutes, until thick. Add vanilla.

<u>Yields: 1 pint</u>

"For 20 years, I tried to make hot fudge sauce that behaved and tasted like perfection and craved and saved for as a child in Milwaukee . . . a thick rich, chocolatey mass that separated into continents when it hit the ice cream . . . yet stayed soft. No luck for 20 years. Perhaps my memory lied. Then I found it. The secret ingredient was evaporated milk."

Desserts

KATHLEEN MATTHEWS is a reporter for WJLA-TV.

Kathleen Matthews
Grapes Grand Marnier

- 1 small bunch seedless green grapes
- 1 ounce Grand Marnier
- 2 tablespoons sugar
- 1 tablespoon sour cream

The grapes should be enough to fill a medium size wine glass. Wash and pluck the grapes off the stems one by one. Discard stems. Pour Grand Marnier into a jar which has a lid. Coat the grapes by turning jar upside down and on its side several times. Soak for 3-4 hours, turning jar every 20 minutes or so. Sprinkle sugar onto a piece of wax paper. Then, drop grapes into the sugar and sprinkle some more sugar on top so they look like little snow balls. Once coated, put the grapes into individual wine glasses or small clear glass bowls. Refrigerate for at least one hour. Just before serving, top with dollop of sour cream. Yes, sour and not whipped cream.

Serves: 1
Increase amounts according to number you want to serve.

"It sounds somewhat bizarre, but I've always had rave reviews. It is very pretty, especially nice for summer because the grapes burst with flavor. The sour cream cuts the sweetness. It is easy to prepare if you are preparing other foods and getting ready for guests. And, you can use the Grand Marnier over again for the same recipe."

Note: We translated this recipe into one serving. But it is really one of those recipes where exact amounts are not important. You can adjust it to suit your tastes."

TONI TRUEBLOOD was a news anchor with WASH-FM when she submitted this recipe. Before coming to Washington she worked in various capacities including anchor, reporter and producer in North Carolina and Indiana.

Toni Trueblood
Ice Cream Angel Food Cake

- 1 angel food cake, homemade or purchased
- 1 quart strawberry ice cream
- 8 ounces Cool Whip

Slice cake in 2 or 3 layers, depending on size of cake. Soften ice cream slightly. Place 1 layer on plate. Spread ice cream evenly over layer. Top with another layer of cake. Repeat if using a third layer. Cover entire cake with Cool Whip. Freeze. Serve frozen.

Variation: Tint Cool Whip pink and top with whole strawberries.

Serves: 6-8

"Quick and easy. Great for summertime entertaining."

HAROLD HOILAND is a photographer with Channel 9's "Eyewitness News." Hal has often impressed his friends and co-workers with his love and knowledge of food and wine.

Harold Hoiland
Irish Coffee Dessert

- 2 envelopes unflavored gelatin
- 1 cup cold milk
- 1 cup milk, heated to boiling
- ⅔ cup sugar
- 2 tablespoons instant coffee powder
- 1 ounce Irish whiskey

1 ounce Creme de Cacao
1 cup heavy cream
1 cup ice cubes (6-8)
  Whipped cream or whipped topping for garnish
  Chocolate curls for garnish

This recipe works best prepared in a blender or food processor.

In a blender container, sprinkle gelatin over cold milk; let stand 3 or 4 minutes. Add hot milk. Cover and blend at stir (low) until gelatin dissolves, about 2 minutes. Add sugar, coffee powder, whiskey and Creme de Cacao. Cover and process on high speed until blended. With blender running, remove feeder cap and add cream and ice cubes one at a time.

Replace cap and continue processing until ice is liquified.

Pour into dessert dishes and chill 30 minutes or until set. Before serving, garnish with whipped cream or whipped topping and chocolate curls.

Serves: 6

GERALD GORDON is a videotape editor in the news department at WDVM-TV. He has worked for Channel 9 for more than 15 years. While Gerry isn't one to spend hours in the kitchen, he says the time it takes to make Kipfel is well worth it.

Gerald Gordon
Kipfel

Dough:
  4 cups flour
  1 teaspoon salt
  1 cup butter
  4 egg yolks, beaten
  1 cup sour cream

Filling:
- ½ pound walnuts or pecans, ground
- 1 cup sugar
- 1 teaspoon cinnamon
- Juice of 1 small lemon
- 4 unbeaten egg whites
- White raisins
- Confectioners sugar for garnish

Sift flour and salt, crumble in butter and mix. Moisten with egg yolks, mixing as you add them. Add sour cream and mix thoroughly. It will make a stiff dough. Knead lightly until smooth. Form into balls that are slightly smaller than walnuts. Refrigerate balls overnight.

The next day, make filling by mixing together filling ingredients, except raisins. Set aside while rolling out dough.

Remove dough from refrigerator and roll or press each ball into flat, thin circle. Spread each with a thin layer of filling and add 5 raisins to each. Roll each and shape into crescents. Bake for about 15 minutes at 350 degrees until light brown. Sprinkle with confectioners sugar while still hot.

Yields: 6-7 dozen

HAROLD HOILAND is a photographer with Channel 9's "Eyewitness News." Hal has often impressed his friends and co-workers with his love and knowledge of food and wine.

Harold Hoiland
Lace Crispies

- ½ cup butter
- 1½ cups old fashioned rolled oats
- ½ cup sugar
- 1 teaspoon baking powder
- ½ teaspoon salt
- 2 teaspoons vanilla
- 1 egg
- 1 cup pecans, chopped

Melt butter and pour over rolled oats. Add sugar, baking powder and salt and blend well.

Add vanilla, egg and nuts. Blend again. Drop by ½ teaspoon, 2½ inches apart on foil-lined cookie sheet. Bake 10-12 minutes at 350 degrees until lightly browned. Cool in refrigerator before removing from foil.

Yields: 6 dozen

SUE ANN STAAKE is a freelance producer and director. She is currently teaching at American University's School of Communication. She has worked for ABC News in Washington, and as a producer/director at WTTG and WDVM-TV.

Sue Ann Staake
Gram Staake's Lebkuchen

- 4 eggs
- 1 pound brown sugar
- 2 cups flour
- 1 teaspoon cinnamon
- 2 ounces citron, cut fine
- 4 ounces blanched almonds, cut fine

Icing:
- 1 cup confectioners sugar
- A few drops vanilla or almond extract
- 2 teaspoons water

Beat eggs with hand mixer. Add brown sugar gradually and beat again. Mix flour and cinnamon with chopped nuts and citron and combine two mixtures. Bake in flat greased baking pans for 25-30 minutes at 375 degrees.

Remove from oven and cool in pans. While cooling, make icing by combining confectioners sugar, water and flavoring to taste, and beat until smooth.

When cool, cut into even strips ½" wide and 5 inches long. Before taking out of pan, frost with icing.

Yields: 2-3 dozen

"Our family's traditional German Christmas treat."

JAN BROWN MCCRACKEN is a parent at the Broadcasters' Child Development Center.

Jan Brown McCracken
Lemon Bars

Crust
- ½ cup butter
- ¼ cup confectioners sugar
- 1 cup flour

Topping
- 2 eggs, beaten
- 2 tablespoons lemon juice
- Grated lemon rind from one lemon
- 1 cup sugar
- 2 tablespoons flour
- ½ teaspoon baking powder

Mix ingredients for crust together and press into 8 inch pan. Bake for 12 minutes at 350. While the mixture is baking, mix together ingredients for topping together. Pour on baked crust and return to oven for 25 minutes more. Cool. Dust with additional confectioners sugar.

MAURY POVICH is anchor/co-anchor of WTTG's "10 O'Clock News" and host of "Panorama." A native Washingtonian, he started his broadcasting career in the mid-60's. He left Washington in 1977 and worked in Chicago, Los Angeles, and Philadelphia before returning to Washington in 1983.

CONNIE CHUNG is anchor of NBC's "News at Sunrise" a correspondent for "American Almanac" and anchor of the weekend newscast for NBC. She began her career at WTTG in Washington and has also worked as a news anchor in Los Angeles. She and Maury Bovich were married in 1984.

<u>Maury Povich and Connie Chung</u>
Povich Family Lemon Meringue Pie

Crust:
- 1½ cups flour
- 1 teaspoon salt
- 6 tablespoons cold butter, cut in pieces
- 3 to 5 tablespoons ice water

Filling:
- ½ cup lemon juice
- 4 egg yolks
- Rind of 2 lemons, grated
- 1 cup sweetened condensed milk

TV Dinners
181

Meringue:
  4 egg whites   ¼ teaspoon cream of tartar   ½ cup sugar

To make crust, mix flour and salt together. Cut in butter, mixing with your fingers or two knives until mixture resembles tiny peas.

Add just enough water to bind mixture. Roll into a ball, wrap in plastic, chill 30 minutes. Roll crust to fit a 9-inch pie plate with an extra 2-inch border. Carefully remove to the plate. Roll the 2 inch border and crimp edges. Weight bottom of crust with dried beans or pie weights. Bake for 25 to 30 minutes at 350 degrees until golden brown. Remove from oven, remove pie weights and cool.

To make filling, beat yolks until thick and lemon-colored. Add remaining filling ingredients and mix well. Set aside.

To make the meringue, beat egg whites until frothy. Add cream of tartar and beat 1 minute. Add sugar a few tablespoons at a time and continue beating until whites are stiff.

To assemble, pour filling into cooked crust. Carefully spoon meringue on top of filling, swirling the tips in a pretty, even pattern. Bake for 15 minutes at 350 degrees or until meringue is nicely browned.

Serves: 8

"This is a Povich family favorite which Maury's mother, Ethyl Povich, got from his sister Lynn a few years ago. Both Maury and Connie rate this recipe high on their list of favorites."

TOM GAUGER joined WMAL radio in 1968 and has filled the mid-day slot since 1970. A native of Florida, he worked there and in North Carolina before coming to Washington. He is a licensed pilot and flies his "Mooney" on weekends.

Tom Gauger
Florida Key Lime Pie

2¼ cups condensed milk
  3 egg yolks

¾ cup plus 2 tablespoons Key Lime juice
8 ounces whipping cream or Cool Whip type topping
1 9-inch pie shell, graham cracker type or baked pastry

In a medium bowl, beat the egg yolks until they are thick and light lemon in color. Using a whisk, blend in the condensed milk. Gradually add lime juice, blending with whisk as you go. The mixture will thicken considerably with the addition of the lime juice. Spoon into pie shell. Refrigerate.

Whip cream until it forms peaks. Chill until ready to serve. Top pie with whipped cream immediately before serving. Pie should not be stored with cream on top.

Serves: 6-8

"It's a terrific pie! Enjoy!"

KEN BEATRICE came to Washington in 1977 and his "You're next on Sports Call" has become his trademark with WMAL listeners. Sports began as a hobby for Ken, but soon led to a career in broadcasting that began in Boston. Ken also enjoys running an independent nationwide collegiate football and basketball scouting organization.

Ken Beatrice
Magic Cookies

½ cup margarine
1½ cups whole graham crackers (about 20)
1 cup walnut pieces
1 6-ounce package chocolate bits
1⅓ cups coconut
1 15-ounce can condensed milk

Melt margarine in 9 × 13 inch ovenproof pan. Grease the sides of pan. Layer dry ingredients in pan in order listed.

Pour condensed milk over the top. Bake for 25 minutes at 350 degrees. Cool and cut in squares.

STEPHANIE CAMPBELL is program manager at WCIX-TV in Miami, Florida. Before leaving Washington last year, she was program director at WDCA-TV and president of the Washington Chapter of N.A.T.A.S. Before coming to Washington she worked in broadcasting in Cincinnati.

Stephanie Campbell
Mecklenburg Pie

Crust:
- 5 ounces pastry mix
- ¼ cup brown sugar
- ½ to ¾ cup pecans, chopped
- 1 ounce semi-sweet chocolate, grated
- 1 teaspoon vanilla
- 1 tablespoon water

Filling:
- ½ cup soft butter
- ¾ cup sugar
- 1 ounce semi-sweet chocolate, melted
- 2 teaspoons instant coffee
- 2 eggs

Topping:
- 2 cups whipped cream
- 2 tablespoons instant coffee
- ½ cup confectioners sugar
- Chocolate curls for garnish

To make pie crust: Combine pastry mix, brown sugar, pecans, grated chocolate, vanilla and water and mix lightly. Pat into aluminum pie pan that has been sprayed with Pam. Bake for 18 minutes at 350 degrees. Set aside and cool.

To make filling: Cream butter, add sugar, gradually blend in coffee and chocolate. Add one egg, beat mixture for 5 minutes. Add second egg and beat 5 minutes more until light and fluffy. Pour in pie shell and refrigerate overnight.

To make topping: Combine topping ingredients and chill for one hour. Beat until stiff peaks form. Refrigerate overnight and put on pie two hours before serving. Garnish with chocolate curls.

Serves: 8

"This recipe came from a now defunct German restaurant in Cincinnati."

Desserts

JIM HOLLINGSWORTH is director of the 6 p.m. and 11 p.m. newscasts at WJLA-TV. Jim found his favorite in the Washington Post.

Jim Hollingsworth
Peanut Butter Fudge

- 3 cups sugar
- ¾ cups butter
- ⅔ cup evaporated milk
- 12 ounces peanut butter morsels
- 7 ounces marshmallow cream
- 1 teaspoon vanilla

In a heavy-gauge saucepan, combine sugar, butter and evaporated milk. Bring to full boil over moderate heat, stirring constantly. Boil 5 minutes, stirring constantly. Remove from heat.

Add peanut butter morsels; stir until they melt and mixture is smooth. Add marshmallow cream and vanilla extract. Beat until well blended. Pour into foil lined 13 × 9 inch pan. Chill until firm.

Yields: 2½ pounds

"The secret to this fudge is the 3 cups of sugar; it gives me just enough energy to direct 1½ hours of live news each day."

SUSAN ALTMAN is producer of WJLA's "Pick Up The Beat" program and of "It's Academic" at WRC-TV.

Susan Altman
Sweet Peach Delight

- 2 peach halves
- 2 tablespoons honey
- 2 ounces rum
- 2 ounces cream or condensed milk

Using your best china or other attractive dish, place 2 peach halves in dish. Add honey, rum and cream.

Serves: 1

"This recipe is great for those who find that chocolate covered cherries do not meet their daily requirement for fruit. It tastes best when served in a romantic setting."

SANDY WEAVER can be heard on Q107 where she has worked for the past 6 years.

Sandy Weaver
Sandy's Pecan Pie

Filling:
- 3 eggs, slightly beaten
- ¾ cup sugar
- ⅛ teaspoon salt
- 1 cup dark corn syrup*
- 1 teaspoon vanilla
- 1 cup pecans, broken in pieces
- 1 cup heavy cream, whipped

Crust:
- 1 cup flour
- ¼ teaspoon salt
- 6 tablespoons cold butter, in small pieces
- 1 egg yolk

*Use slightly less than the one cup of dark corn syrup. The pie filling sets up better with less corn syrup.

Preheat oven to 400°F.

Mix the flour and salt in a bowl. Cut in the butter with your fingers or a pastry blender until the mixture resembles coarse meal or tiny peas. Whisk the egg yolk and 2 tablespoons water together in another bowl, add to the flour mixture, and blend until the pastry is smooth and holds together in a ball. It can be mixed in a food processor, process first the flour, salt and butter quickly together, then add the egg yolk and water through the funnel and process until the dough balls up around the blade. Wrap in foil or plastic and refrigerate for at least 20 minutes. You can roll this dough out with a rolling pin, but you have to chill it, wrapped in plastic for at least 20 minutes. Using the heal of your hands, pull pieces of dough from the ball and press them over the bottom and sides of the pan. The dough should be thick enough to hold the filling, but be careful that it is not too thick around the bottom edge or the finished tart will seem coarse. If there's time, cover the lined pan snugly with foil and refrigerate it before filling and baking it.

Line a 9-inch _glass_ pie pan with the pastry dough. Combine the eggs, sugar, salt, corn syrup, and vanilla in a bowl and blend well. Stir in the pecans. Pour into the lined pan. Bake for 10 minutes, then reduce the heat to 325°F and bake for another 35 minutes. Serve with unsweetened whipped cream.

***Note: Do not overwork the pastry.

FRED KNIGHT is currently devoting his energies to a full time career in managing his doughnut business. For many years, he was a familiar face to Washington viewers as a weatherman at WTTG and at WDVM-TV.

Fred Knight
Pineapple Bake

½ cup butter
1 cup sugar
4 eggs

2½ cups crushed pineapple
6 pieces bread, cut in cubes

Cream butter and sugar together. Add eggs and beat well. Add pineapple and fold in bread cubes. Bake in greased casserole uncovered for 1 hour at 350 degrees or until lightly browned. Serve hot or cold.

Serves: 6

"It's fabulous."

JANET TERRY is a newswriter for WDVM-TV's Eyewitness News.

Janet Terry
Sweet Potato Pie

 4 large sweet potatoes, mashed
 ¾ cup pineapple juice
 1 teaspoon vanilla
 4 tablespoons butter
 2 tablespoons flour
 1 teaspoon baking soda
 1 tablespoon lemon rind
 ½ cup sugar
 2 eggs
 1 unbaked 9 inch pie shell

Boil sweet potatoes in skins until soft. Peel off skins and mash in large bowl. Mix potatoes together with all other ingredients until well blended. Pour into pie shell and bake for 45 minutes at 375 degrees.

Serves: 8

WILLARD SCOTT is best known as the zany weatherman on NBC's "Today Show." But before joining the show, he spent many years in Washington as weatherman for WRC-TV and as part of the popular "Joy Boys" radio team. He also has the distinction of selling fresh eggs to his fellow employees at WRC ... eggs which he transported with care from his farm in Virginia. (*See Willard's photo in the main course section with his recipe for Cheese Grits Souffle.*)

Willard Scott
Brown Sugar Pound Cake

 1 cup butter
 ½ cup Crisco shortening
 5 eggs
 3½ cups plain flour

 1 pound plus 1 cup light brown sugar
 ½ teaspoon baking powder
 1 cup milk

Frosting:
- ½ cup butter
- 1 cup pecans, chopped
- 1 16-ounce box confectioners sugar
- Milk to thin

Let eggs and butter set until they are room temperature. Cream butter and Crisco. Add eggs, one at a time, creaming after each. Add brown sugar and mix well. Sift flour and baking powder. Add flour-baking powder mixture alternately with milk to sugar mixture. Bake in greased and floured tube pan for 1¼ to 1½ hours at 325 degrees.

To make frosting: Toast pecans in oven along with butter in thick broiler pan until they brown well. Let cool a little, then add box of confectioners sugar and mix. Add enough milk to thin to spreading consistency. Spread on top of cake. Some icing should "drip" down sides and center, but spread only on top.

Serves: 8-10

MADILEE WNEK writes editorials for WJLA-TV as well as freelance articles for newspapers and magazines.

Madilee Wnek
Pound Cake

- 1½ cups butter or margarine
- 1 16-ounce box confectioners sugar
- 6 eggs
- 1 teaspoon lemon extract
- 1 teaspoon vanilla
- 3 cups Gold Medal flour

Cream butter and sugar together. Add one egg at a time, beating after each addition. Add lemon extract and vanilla. Add flour gradually. Pour batter into tube or bundt pan that has been greased with butter and dusted with flour. Bake for 1 hour and 25 minutes at 325 degrees.

Serves: 8-10

"This is the best pound cake I've ever tasted. The recipe has been in my family for decades. It is especially scrumptious served with butter while still warm."

BILL KURTIS is a news anchor in Chicago and former co-anchor of the CBS Morning News. His work with CBS News often brought him to Washington.

Bill Kurtis
Raspberry Tart

Shell:
- 2 cups flour
- ¼ teaspoon salt
- 2 tablespoons sugar
- 12 tablespoons cold butter
- 2 egg yolks
- 2-4 tablespoons ice water

Pastry Cream:
- 1½ cups whole milk
- ½ cup heavy cream
- 4 egg yolks
- ½ cup sugar
- 3 tablespoons cornstarch
- 1 teaspoon vanilla

Topping:
- 2-3 cups raspberries
- ¼ cup raspberry jam (optional)
- 2 tablespoons water, heated (optional)

To make shell: Combine flour, salt and sugar. Cut in butter with pastry blender to texture of coarse corn meal. Beat yolks and water together and add, stirring quickly with fork. Gather dough into a ball. Chill one hour.

Preheat oven to 400 degrees. Roll out dough. Line a 10 inch tart shell, preferably with removable bottom. Line dough with waxed paper and add dried peas or aluminum pellets. Place on baking sheet and bake 20 minutes. Remove peas or pellets and paper. Reduce oven to 375 degrees and continue baking 15 minutes longer or until golden brown. Cool.

To prepare filling: Mix milk and cream in pan, bring to boil. Meanwhile mix egg yolks and sugar until pale yellow. Add cornstarch to yolk mix and beat well. Add remaining ½ cup milk and beat. When milk and cream mixture is at a boil, remove from heat, and add yolk mixture, beating rapidly with a wire whisk. Return to heat, bring to boil stirring constantly with whisk. When thickened, and at the boil, remove from heat, add vanilla and let cool.

To assemble tart: Fill cooled tart shell with pastry cream. Cover top of cream with 2-3 cups raspberries. Can be served as is, or glazed with raspberry jam that has been heated with 2 tablespoons of water and brushed on raspberries.

Serves: 8

KATHLEEN SULLIVAN co-anchors ABC News' "World News This Morning" and anchors "World News Saturday." She joined ABC in 1982 after working for Cable News Network. A native of California, she began her career in 1977 in Los Angeles.

Kathleen Sullivan
Refrigerator Cake

1 pint whipping cream
1 box chocolate wafers
Vanilla, to taste
Sprinkles of confectioners sugar
2 ounces creme de menthe (optional)

Whip cream in heavy bowl. Add vanilla and or creme de menthe and sugar to taste. With spatula, cover each chocolate wafer with ½ inch thick whipped cream and stack in rows in pan of choice. When pan is filled, cover entire surface with remaining whipped cream. Sprinkle top with crushed chocolate crumbs. Refrigerate and serve in bowls or on plates.

Serves: 4-6

"My mother taught me to make this when I was six and it still tastes as good to me now as the first time I made it. It is great for last minute entertaining."

ANDREA WILLIAMS is administrative assistant for Q107's general manager. She is also a parent at the Broadcasters' Child Development Center.

Andrea Williams
Rum Balls

- 2 cups confectioners sugar
- 3 tablespoons unsweetened cocoa powder
- ½ cup dark Jamaican rum
- ¼ cup light corn syrup
- 3½ cups vanilla wafers, crushed
- 1 cup pecans, walnuts or almonds, finely chopped
- ½- 1 cup confectioners sugar for rolling balls when finished

Sift sugar and cocoa in large mixing bowl. Stir in rum and corn syrup until blended. Stir in wafer crumbs and nuts; mix until well blended. Shape small amount of mixture into 1-inch balls. Roll in the additional confectioners sugar. Store in tightly covered container. Omit rum if preparing for children.

Yields: 3-4 dozen

"If wrapped well and stored in tightly covered container, rum balls will keep for weeks."

STAN GUTTENBERG is an engineer at WDVM-TV. He credits his wife Harriet for this recipe.

Stan Guttenberg
Sherry Cake

- 1 package yellow cake mix
- 1½ packages instant butterscotch pudding mix
- 2½-3 ounces poppy seeds
- 1 cup cream sherry
- 1 cup salad oil
- 4 eggs

Place all ingredients in a large bowl. Stir until all ingredients are moistened. Beat well for 2 minutes. Pour into greased angel food or bundt pan. Bake for 60-75 minutes at 375 degrees or until toothpick comes out clean.

Serves: 8-10

"It is one of my favorites to eat, not prepare. My wife Harriet gets all the credit as chef."

KATHY FILOSI NELSON is a field producer and writer for NBC News' "Today Show." She is also a parent at the Broadcasters' Child Development Center and president of its Board of Directors.

Kathy Filosi Nelson
English Butter Toffee

- 1 cup sugar
- 1 cup unsalted butter
- ¼ cup water
- ½ teaspoon salt
- 1 teaspoon vanilla
- 4-6 ounces milk chocolate
- 4-6 ounces bittersweet chocolate
- 1 pound walnuts, finely chopped

Combine sugar, butter, water and salt in saucepan over medium heat. Bring to boil, stirring constantly. Boil to hard crack 305 degrees. It will take a long time, but don't get impatient. Remove immediately. Stir in vanilla. Pour toffee into buttered cookie sheet. Cool in refrigerator until hard. In the meantime, melt both types of chocolate in top of double boiler. When toffee hardens, evenly brush top with one half of chocolate. Cover with ½ of nuts and pat nuts into chocolate. Cool in refrigerator until cool and hard. When completely hardened, invert into a second buttered cookie sheet. Repeat procedure with remaining chocolate and nuts. Cool until hard, crack into pieces and store in airtight container or refrigerator.

"This is time consuming, but worth it! The secret . . . the better the chocolate, the better the candy. It makes a great present at Christmas!"

CAROL POWELL is production manager for WJLA-TV.

Carol Powell
English Toffee Cookies

- 1 cup butter
- 1 egg yolk, beaten
- 1 teaspoon vanilla
- 1 cup brown sugar
- 2 cups flour
- 6 ounces sweet chocolate
- 1 cup chopped nuts

Blend butter, sugar, and egg yolks until smooth. Add flour and vanilla. Spread mixture thinly over large cookie sheet. Bake for 15 to 20 minutes at 350 degrees. Melt chocolate and spread over cookie while hot. Sprinkle with chopped nuts. Cut in squares before dough hardens and cool on wire rack.

Yield: approximately 2 dozen

"This recipe was given to me by my grandmother."

SCOTT WOODSIDE is half of the popular Elliott and Woodside team at Q107 where he has worked since 1982. Prior to joining the station he worked at WPGC where he teamed up with Jim Elliott in 1978. His radio career began in 1965 and has also included work in Atlanta, Georgia before coming to Washington.

Scott Woodside
Toffee Bars

- 1 cup granulated sugar
- 1 cup butter—must be butter, not a substitute!
- 1 egg yolk, well beaten
- 2 cups flour
- ¾ pound Hershey bar, broken in small pieces
- ½- ¾ cups chopped nuts (optional)

Mix together sugar, butter and egg yolk until well blended. Add flour and mix well. Spread on 12 × 15 cookie sheet—the kind with sides. Pat down with hands to spread evenly over entire pan. Bake for 15 minutes at 350 degrees. Remove from oven and spread immediately with Hershey Bar pieces. Sprinkle with nuts if desired. Cool. Cut in strips.

Yield: 2 dozen

THE LEFTOVERS
BREADS, BEVERAGES & OTHERS

Beverages

MYLA LERNER is a parent at the Broadcasters' Child Development Center.

Myla Lerner
Banana-Orange Frosted

- 1 ripe banana
- ½ cup orange juice
- ½ cup cold milk
- ½ pint (1 cup) orange sherbet

Slice ripe banana and mash with fork. Add orange juice and beat until smooth. Add milk and sherbet. Beat again until smooth. Pour into glasses. Top each glass with additional scoop of orange sherbet, if desired.

Serves: 2-3

"Great for those miserable summer nights."

JAN THOMPSON is senior producer and segment host for WDVM's "Capital Edition." Before joining Channel 9 in 1983, she worked as a reporter and anchor in Cincinnati and as executive producer of a syndicated program. (*See Jan's photo in the Appetizer section with her recipe for Tri-Color Pasta Salad.*)

Jan Thompson
Bourbon Slush

- 1 cup boiling water
- 5 tea bags
- 5 cups 7-Up
- 1 cup bourbon
- 1 12-ounce can frozen orange juice concentrate
- 1 6-ounce can frozen lemonade concentrate
- 1 cup sugar

Add tea bags to water and brew until tea is dark, strong tea. Mix with rest of ingredients until well blended and smooth. Place in freezer until consistency of slush.

Serves: 2 lushes

KATHY BLUNT is host of Channel 20's "Eye on Washington." Her Washington TV experience also includes several years at WTTG.

Kathy Blunt
Fantastic Holiday Eggnog

- 12 eggs
- 1½ cups sugar
- 1/5 th dark rum
- 1 quart milk
- 6 egg whites
- 2 pints whipping cream
- Sprinkles of freshly grated nutmeg

Separate egg whites from yolks, save egg whites for use later. Beat yolks until bright yellow. Add sugar, beat until stiff, about 2 or 3 minutes. Add rum and milk and stir until well blended.

Beat all the egg whites until peaks form. Fold egg whites into mixture and chill for 2 hours, preferably outside if it is cold enough. Whip cream until creamy, but not too thick. Add to mixture and chill for another 2 hours. Grate fresh nutmeg on top and serve.

Serves: 12-16

"It is fantastic. Enjoy."

BOB McBRIDE retired this year after more than 30 years in journalism. He joined WRC-TV in 1982 as a co-anchor of the 6 p.m. and 1 p.m. newscasts. Prior to his work at Channel 4, he held several management positions including General Manager at WJBK-TV in Detroit; anchored the news for WBBM-TV in Chicago; and worked for Detroit Free Press and as a radio reporter based in Washington.

Bob McBride
My Irish Grandmother's Tea Mix . . . A Modern Instant Non-Alcoholic Version

- 1 cup instant tea (preferably sweetened with lemon flavor added)
- 1 cup orange Tang
- 1 generous teaspoon cinnamon
- 1 generous teaspoon ground cloves

Mix all ingredients together and store in covered glass jar.

To make 1 cup of tea, use 2 or 3 teaspoons to 1 cup boiling water.

"Adjust spices and amount used for each serving to your own personal tastes. It tastes best served in stoneware or ceramic mug."

VALERIE GIBSON is a teacher in the infant section of the Broadcasters' Child Development Center.

Valerie Gibson
Tangy Lime Punch

- 2 6-ounce cans frozen lime drink
- 1 12-ounce can frozen lemonade concentrate
- 2 cups pineapple juice
- 2 cups water
- ½ cup lemon juice
- 2 quarts club soda, chilled
- Ice cubes

Combine lime drink mix, lemonade, pineapple juice, water and lemon juice. Chill. Just before serving, add club soda and ice cubes.

Serves: 8-10

BREADS

RUBY TAKANISHI is a parent at the Broadcasters' Child Development Center.

Ruby Takanishi
Kauai Banana Bread

- 2 cups unbleached flour
- 1¼ cups sugar
- 2 teaspoons baking soda
- 1 teaspoon cinnamon
- 2 eggs
- 3 large very soft bananas
- ½ cup vegetable oil
- ½ cup butter or margarine, melted
- 1 teaspoon vanilla

Combine flour, sugar, baking soda, cinnamon and mix together in large bowl. In separate bowl, combine eggs, bananas, oil, margarine, vanilla and blend thoroughly. Combine the dry ingredients with the egg-banana mixture and mix well. Pour mixture into a 9 × 5 inch bread pan that has been rubbed with oil and lined with wax paper. Bake for 1 hour at 350 degrees.

Yield: 1 loaf

"This recipe produces a dark brown banana bread that is unique in taste and texture. It is best when aged 1 or 2 days before serving, if you can wait. Freezes well. Great for gift giving."

STEVE HAGEDORN is a writer and producer for WDCA's Promotion Department.

Steve Hagedorn
Bran Muffins

- 5 cups flour
- 3 cups sugar
- 1 15-ounce package Raisin Bran flakes
- 5 teaspoons baking soda
- 2 teaspoons salt
- 1 cup raisins
- 1 quart buttermilk
- 4 eggs, lightly beaten
- 1 cup vegetable oil

Leftovers

Combine flour, sugar, raisin bran flakes, baking soda, salt and raisins. Mix well. In a separate bowl, combine buttermilk, eggs and oil and mix well. Combine buttermilk mixture with dry ingredients and mix just until blended. Cover and refrigerate overnight. When ready to bake, preheat oven to 400 degrees. Grease muffin tins and fill ¾ full. Bake 20 minutes.

Yields: 4-5 dozen

"Dough will keep for up to 6 weeks in refrigerator."

STEPHANIE WILSON is a production assistant for WDVM-TV's "Capital Edition."

Stephanie S. Wilson
Pumpkin Bread

- 4 cups flour
- 3 cups sugar
- 2 teaspoons baking soda
- ½ teaspoon salt
- 1 teaspoon baking powder
- 1 teaspoon cinnamon
- 1 teaspoon nutmeg
- ½ teaspoon allspice
- ½ teaspoon cloves, ground
- ¼ teaspoon ginger
- 1 cup vegetable oil
- 1 16-ounce can pumpkin
- ⅔ cup cold water
- 4 eggs
- 1 cup chopped pecans

Preheat oven to 350 degrees.

Sift together first 10 ingredients. Make a well in mixture and add oil, pumpkin and cold water. Blend very well with electric mixer. Add eggs one at a time, beating after each one. Fold in pecans. Pour batter into greased, floured loaf pans. Bake for 1 hour. Cool on wire racks.

Yields: 3 loaves

"This recipe has been handed down for generations in our family and is a Thanksgiving and Christmas specialty. This bread freezes well."

LAUREN WERNER is a videotape editor with WDVM-TV's Eyewitness News. She enjoys experimenting with new recipes and also likes to look for antiques in her spare time.

Lauren Werner
Lemon Popovers

- 4 eggs
- 2 cups milk
- 2 cups all purpose flour
- 1 teaspoon salt
- Grated peel of ½ lemon

Preheat oven to 375 degrees. Important!

In a small bowl, beat eggs and milk until smooth. In another bowl, stir flour and salt together; make a well in center and pour egg mixture into it. Then beat with egg beater, or electric mixer about 1 minute or until batter is smooth and thin. Grease a 12-muffin muffin pan, or 12 custard cups, very well. Fill cups half full with batter. Bake for 30 minutes in preheated oven. DO NOT OPEN DOOR. Turn heat down to 350 degrees and bake 30-35 minutes longer or until well browned. Serve hot with butter and jam.

Yield: 12

RENEE ANTOSH is an account executive with WTTG and a parent at the Broadcasters' Child Development Center.

Renee Antosh
Parmesan Popovers

- ¼ cup parmesan cheese, freshly grated
- 1 cup milk
- 1 cup all purpose flour
- 1 tablespoon butter, melted
- ¼ teaspoon salt
- 2 large eggs

Preheat oven to 450 degrees. Grease 6 deep muffin pans or custard cups and sprinkle with parmesan. Set aside.

Combine milk, flour, butter and salt in medium bowl. Beat in eggs just until blended. Overbeating will reduce volume. Fill cups ¾ cups full. Bake 15 minutes. Reduce heat to 350 degrees. DO NOT OPEN OVEN DOOR. Bake 20 minutes more. Carefully remove popovers from pan with spatula and serve warm.

A Step By Step Guide For Making Bread

DAN ALEXANDER is the morning drive man for Europe at Voice of America. He is better known to his family and friends as Michael Wolfgang. He has worked in broadcasting for more than 25 years including positions at Q107 in Washington. He has been both a DJ and production director and has worked in every format except classical.

Dan Alexander
All Natural Lite Brown Bread

- 2 cups whole milk
- 3 tablespoons butter, do not substitute margarine
- 3 tablespoons honey
- 1 tablespoon salt
- 2 tablespoons yeast
- ⅓ cup lukewarm water
- ½ cup wheat germ
- 3¼ cups of all purpose white flour <u>and</u>
- 3¼ cups of whole wheat flour <u>well-mixed together in separate bowl</u>

First: Scald the milk. (You can also scold it but it won't pay any attention.) The milk has reached the scalding point <u>just</u> as it begins to boil. Remove from heat and add to it the butter, salt and honey. Pour into a large mixing bowl and let cool to lukewarm.

Next: Dissolve the yeast in the lukewarm water . . . wait a few minutes . . . (you're allowing the milk mixture to cool off to a lukewarm temperature.) . . . then add the dissolved yeast into the lukewarm milk. Yeast, being the temperamental little buggers they are, hate temperature extremes. If in doubt as to the tepid nature of the milk . . . check it out with your elbow . . . preferably with the sleeve rolled up.

Then: Add the wheat germ and about three cups of the flour mixture to the milk mixture, stirring vigorously with a wooden spoon until the batter is smooth. Add more flour and keep stirring until the dough is too stiff to stir with the spoon. (You may not use all the flour . . . add remaining flour slowly . . . put extra aside for possible use in the kneading process . . . which brings us to . . .

The Kneading Process: Turn dough out onto a floured board and knead—adding more flour as necessary to keep it from sticking—until it is very smooth and elastic.

... (meanwhile) ... Have a buttered bowl standing by ... remember: if all goes well and your yeast is/are happy, the dough will expand to twice its size!!

Post-Kneading: Turn dough into the buttered bowl ... flip it over (This places a thin coating of butter over the entire surface of the dough.) ... cover the bowl with a towel. Leave it in a warm place to rise until double in bulk—about one hour. Punch it down ... (Lovingly, please!) ... cover ... and allow it to rise again.

The Kneading Process (Part Two): Pour dough onto board and gently knead again a few times ... divide into two equal balls of dough ... shape each into loaves ...

... (meanwhile) ... Have two standard bread pans, well-buttered, standing by.

Then: Place the loaves into the bread pans ... cover with the towel ... and leave them to rise again until almost double—about 45 minutes at the most.

30 Minutes Later: Preheat oven to 375 degrees. (Make sure middle rack is in place.)

Finally: Bake loaves for 45 minutes. The final product should emerge golden brown. Gently shake loaves out of their respective pans onto the board. Place pans on top of the stove, carefully replacing loaves cross-wise atop the pans to cool. Immediately slather the crust with butter prior to cooling. Once bread has cooled somewhat ... but is still quite warm ... try a generously buttered slice covered with your favorite jam, honey, peanut butter, etc.

Some bachelor's suggest:

UNCLE JOHNNY was with Q107 when he submitted this recipe. It is guaranteed never to fail.

Uncle Johnny
Bachelor's Linguini

Although I can't cook, I have an excellent recipe for Linguini in Red Clam Sauce. Get in car and drive to the Roma Restaurant on Connecticut Avenue. Get out of the car and walk into restaurant. Tell the waitress you want linguini with red clam sauce. When she brings it get ready to say, "Wow! This looks great!!!!" Don't forget to tell them Uncle Johnny sent you."

ARTHUR STEADMAN is a news writer for WDVM-TV.

Arthur Steadman
L'il Pizzas

The rigors of bachelor life require meals that are quick, cheap, filling, and guaranteed to make your mother cry if she knew. My favorite is L'il Pizzas.
1. Cut open an English muffin.
2. Toast it to taste.
3. Dump jarred tomato sauce of choice on the muffin halves.
4. Dump mozzarella cheese on the sauce.
5. Place in toaster oven (on bake) for 15 minutes or until the smoke alarm goes off. 500 degrees is best.
6. Remove and eat.

The beauty of L'il Pizzas is that if you have friends over, you can make each little one to taste. (Lots of sauce vs. hardly any, etc.) Your friends might also feel sorry for you and take you out to dinner.

Helpful hints: Don't bake ALL your pizzas at same time. They are deceptively filling . . . and unused, uncooked pizzas can be popped into a plastic sandwich bag and slipped in the freezer, or just the fridge.

Unused COOKED pizzas can be frozen and reheated up to months later.

Frozen pizzas can be used as projectiles when the drunks pour out of the local tavern at 3 a.m. and wake you up.

"I like MY L'il Pizzas best with a can of beer during the Sunday morning Tarzan movies on Channel 20."

NOTE: *Sometimes the author cooks his pizzas at only 400 degrees for 20-25 minutes. That allows a quick shower and a cigarette while cooking.*

TOD MESIROW is a segment producer for WDVM's "Capital Edition." He claims he lived on this recipe while a starving college student in London.

Tod Mesirow
London Poverty Mush

- 1 cup cooked rice
- ½ cup peas, cooked
- 1 tablespoon butter or margarine
- ½ cup mushrooms, sliced
- ¼ cup white wine
- Garlic, to taste
- Oregano, to taste
- White pepper, to taste
- ½ cup cheddar cheese, grated

Cook rice and set aside. In a skillet, melt butter. Add mushrooms and saute until brown. Add wine and spices to suit your taste. Combine this mixture with rice, peas, and grated cheese.

Serves: 1 starving student

"As a poverty stricken college student in London, I ate this mush more often than I'd like to remember. It is actually quite good and can easily be adjusted to suit your tastes or available ingredients."

BERNIE SMILOVITZ is WTTG's sports director prior to joining Changel 5, he worked at WTOP radio. When he submitted this recipe, he was a bachelor.

Bernie Smilovitz
How to Boil Water

"Get a pot, put some water in it. Turn on the burner and put the pot on it. When the water starts to bubble, it is boiling. you can add instant coffee or instant soup . . . YUMMY!"

LARRY SHAINMAN is a reporter at WRC-TV.

Larry Shainman
Don't Cook!

"As a lifelong bachelor, my diet consists largely of Kraft Macaroni Dinner, steaks at Clyde's and cheeseburgers from Timberlake's on Connecticut Avenue."

SUSAN KING is a news anchor for Channel 4's 6 p.m. newscast. Her cover "Susan King's Cover Story" airs nightly on the 11 p.m. newscast. She is often faced with preparing dinner for guests between the two programs. (See photo and additional bio information in the Maincourse section with Susan's recipe for "Emmies Chicken".

Susan King
Dinner Between the Six and Eleven

Dilema. Guests are coming from out of town who don't realize that the T.V. business means you are always against the clock and that weekends don't start at 6:00 p.m. on Friday night. Weekends begin when you get off.

The question is how can you prepare a dinner that looks like you are the epitome of hospitality without any work.

The answer is do it ahead and do it simple. Mainly because in the news business you may not even get home after the six to join them all at your feast.

This dinner is not going to put you in the annals of gourmet magazine but its a tried and true favorite that assures you your understanding husband can pull it off without you, and that he won't have to call for directions for the complicated dish only you know how to prepare.

We call it French Peasant Chicken. It's an old fashioned chicken in the pot that steams for a day and gives your house the aroma of a non-tv at home hosst.

All you need is one crock pot, a half dozen chicken breasts and thighs, (you can use a small whole chicken but we find the larger meatier pieces easier to serve) carrots, onions and celery. Line the crock pot early in the day (before you even face the newsroom) with carrots. Cut in edible chunk size. Add the chicken to the pot, sliced celery and chunks of onions. Pour in a cup of white wine, a teaspoon of oregano, 2 teaspoons of basil, (this is the secret ingredient) pinch of rosemary and lots of pepper. Cook on low for at least 8-10 hours.

The chicken gets a rich flavorable taste and should be served over rice. A mixed green salad with artichokes compliments the chicken and vegetable main course. French bread is a must.

The beauty of this meal is that it is all ready when you come home after the six, all you need to do is boil the water for rice while you join your guests for some cheese, a drink and catch up. If you set the table in the morning there is no preparation when you arrive and getting back to do the eleven is easy. You can leave the dishes for the impressed guests to do because there's really only two pots—the crock and rice pot. This is also a dinner that doesn't demand too much wine drinking so you can be sure your guests will stay up and watch you do the eleven!

JOHN O. GOLDSMITH is host of "Capital Edition" on WDVM-TV. His work at Channel 9 is a return engagement at the station where he worked as a reporter from 1979 to 1982. John's career spans 24 years and includes many years as a news anchor at WTTG and later worked as a reporter at at station. He also worked for WWDC early in his career and owned his own production company specializing in documentaries.

John O. Goldsmith
Flash and Trash Dining

A "junk food" aficionado from way back, your author has dined in such four star, gourmet, eateries as: the WWDC Radio lunchroom (when its studios were on Brookville Road across from "the dump"), the WTTG-TV dining facility (when it was a fast food joint called "Dave's Cave") and now WDVM's luxurious mechanical restaurant (which is called "The TOP Room" but is situated at the bottom of the building.) In fact, all of these emporiums of gastronomical delight, for some reason, have been located in basements.

Two rules for meals from machine: before committing coins, **always** check the date on the sandwich package. Because only the month and the day are specified, this won't help you if the tuna salad was prepared in a prior **year** but then you are protected by rule number two: **never** buy **anything** that moves.

I favor items that require reheating because the microwaves will kill almost everything . . . except for bad taste. Always take the innards out of the sandwich and heat them first. Then replace them in the bread and briefly zap the dickens out of that sucker. Otherwise, by the time the innards are hot the bread has taken on the consistency of a Goodyear radial.

Leftovers

My favorite meals change with the whims of our food supplier but right now I'm partial to:

Appetizer:
Chicken Noodle Soup a la Campbell's
(... because it's a known commodity.)

Entree:
Egg 'n Salami Surprise on an English Muffin
(... the "surprise" is: it ain't half bad!)

Dessert:
Passion Fruit Yogurt
(... which makes me believe I'm having a healthy meal.)

A "Butterfinger" Bar
(... which I don't like but that's what our candy machine gives you when you ask for a "Payday.")

P.S.
Proper microwave etiquette calls for covering food with a paper plate or napkin prior to heating. Otherwise the next chef will find an oven interior that looks like it was just used to execute a hamster.

"Bon Appetit"

ED TURNEY is best known for his "Turney's World" on WJLA-TV newscasts. His career at WJLA and in Washington broadcasting spans more than 2 decades.

Ed Turney
Cookin' Live Crabs ... Like a Pro

Take the bottom of a 2 section crab pot and fill bottom with about ½ inch to 1½ inches of a mixture of half water and half beer. You can substitute vinegar for the beer, or you can use all water if you don't want any beer or vinegar smell in the kitchen. Sometimes, 1 12-ounce can of beer can add quite a bit of flavor. Then, get yourself some live crabs ... remember, if they ain't kickin, you ain't cookin. In the top section of pot, put live crabs in layers and sprinkle each layer with "hot sauce." Usually the best is the stuff sold where you buy the crabs or you can mix it up yourself. If you decide to make it yourself, use coarse salt, some seafood seasoning and bunch of cayenne pepper. Use the trial and error method and suit your own taste.

Bring water in bottom section of pot to boil. As soon as you get a heavy steam, put top section of pot containing crabs over the bottom section. Cover and cook ½ hour. Many people say 20 minutes, but I like 30 minutes best. Remove crabs from pot and put on paper-covered table. Never, never use a tablecloth, it is bad taste. Insert crabs in stomach. Refrigerate left-over crabs and pick next day ... put some crab meat in frying pan with butter and brown ... yum, yum, yum, and then some.

"P.S. A tip to the trashmen will be appreciated!"

JOHN DOUGLASS is on the faculty of American University's School of Communication where he heads the graduate film and video production program. He is the current President of the Washington Chapter of N.A.T.A.S. and a parent at the Broadcasters' Child Development Center.

John Douglass
Easy Granola

4 cups oats
2 cups wheat germ
1 cup coconut
1 cup nuts, chopped
1 cup sesame seeds or sunflower seeds
¾ cup vegetable oil
⅓ cup water
2 teaspoons vanilla

Combine all ingredients and mix well. Bake for 1 hour at 350 degrees, stirring frequently.

PAUL FINE is a producer and photographer for "CBS Reports" and "60 Minutes." Before joining CBS, he teamed up with his wife Holly Fine for many years at WJLA-TV.

Paul Fine
Harvest Popcorn

⅓ cup butter or margarine, melted
1 teaspoon dried dillweed
1 teaspoon lemon pepper
1 teaspoon worcestershire sauce
½ teaspoon garlic powder
½ teaspoon onion powder
¼ teaspoon salt
2 quarts popcorn, popped
(⅓ *cup unpopped kernels makes about 2½ quarts popped corn*)
2 cups shoestring potatoes
1 cup mixed nuts

Preheat oven to 350 degrees.
Mix butter, dillweed, lemon pepper, worcestershire sauce, garlic powder, onion powder and salt. Toss with remaining ingredients. Spread popcorn mixture in jelly roll pan. Bake for 6 to 8 minutes. Stir once while baking.

Yields: 2½ quarts

This recipe was submitted by the staff of Broadcasters' Child Development Center. While it is not meant to be eaten, there is nothing in it that would hurt anyone if they did.

BCDC Favorite Playdough

- 1 cup flour
- ½ cup salt
- 2 tablespoons cream of tartar
- 1 tablespoon vegetable oil
- 1 cup water
- A few drops food coloring, if desired

Mix all ingredients together in a saucepan. Cook over medium heat stirring constantly until mixture thickens and is the consistency of playdough. Turn out of the pan onto the counter. Knead while warm to remove lumps if necessary.

Store in an airtight container.

<u>Yields: Enough for</u> lots of fun for 2 or 3 children

"This is the playdough used at BCDC and is well tested for durability by numerous toddlers and preschoolers. Stored in an airtight container, the playdough will keep for 2 to 3 months."

GENA FITZGERALD is a producer for News 7's investigative unit. She has worked at WJLA since 1978. When she isn't digging up stories, she's doing volunteer work with the Alexandria Urban Archeology Program.

Gena Fitzgerald
Instant Italian

- 4 tablespoons oregano
- 4 tablespoons onion flakes
- 4 tablespoons parsley
- 4 teaspoons marjoram
- 4 teaspoons basil
- 4 teaspoons garlic flakes
- 2 teaspoons thyme
- 2 teaspoons rosemary
- 3 bay leaves
- 1 teaspoon celery seed
- 2 teaspoons fresh ground pepper

In a medium bowl, combine all ingredients. With a mortar and pestle crush the mixture a few teaspoons at a time until well blended. Store in a shaker container.

Yield: 1 cup

This is an all purpose seasoning mix. Shake on top of chicken or fish for a salt-free seasoning.

Use as the seasoning for homemade spaghetti sauce or to make store bought sauce taste a bit more homemade.

For an instant and easy Italian salad dressing, mix: 1 teaspoon of seasoning with ½ cup olive oil and 2 tablespoons red wine vinegar.

Measurements And Equivalents

Liquid And Dry Measure Equivalents

  a pinch = slightly less than ⅛ teaspoon
  a dash = a few drops
  3 teaspoons = 1 tablespoon
  4 tablespoons = ¼ cup
5⅓ tablespoons = ⅓ cup
  8 tablespoons = ½ cup
16 tablespoons = 1 cup
  2 tablespoons (liquid) = 1 ounce
  1 cup = 8 fluid ounces
  2 cups = 1 pint (16 fluid ounces)
  4 cups = 1 quart (32 fluid ounces)

Other Equivalents

1 stick butter or margarine = ¼ pound = 8 tablespoons = ½ cup
4 ounces cheddar or american cheese = 1 cup grated cheese
8 ounces sour cream = 1 cup sour cream
8 ounces whipping or heavy cream = ½ pint = 2 cups whipped cream
1 lemon = 2 to 3 tablespoons juice
1 lemon = 2 teaspoons grated rind
1 orange = ⅓ to ½ cups juice
1 orange = 2-3 tablespoons grated rind
1 pound carrots = 3 to 4 cups shredded carrots
1 pound (16-ounce package) confectioners sugar = 3½ cups
1 pound brown sugar = 2¼ cups, packed
1 pound granulated sugar = 2 cups
1 pound sifted flour = approximately 4 cups

About N.A.T.A.S.

The National Academy of Television Arts and Sciences is dedicated to excellence in the broadcast industry. It is the only organization that cuts across the lines of management and craft in representing the industry; that represents broadcast personnel as well as independent producers, advertisers, educators and students.

NATAS awards the Emmy in recognition of excellence. Any group of people can get together, pat themselves on the back and tell the rest of the world how great they are. That is not the purpose of this organization. We reward excellence in an effort to promote excellence. Free speech and a free press is guaranteed. But the quality of the voice and news coverage is not. Awarding the Emmy helps.

NATAS helps in other ways as well. We created and continue to support through projects such as this cookbook one of the finest day care centers in the Washington area, the Broadcasters' Child Development Center. And since this center cannot serve all our members, NATAS has a fund to provide support to single parents and others working in the industry who have difficulty paying the high cost of child care.

NATAS provides scholarship awards for area college and university students. These are competitive, based on a student's ideas for a community service or public service campaign. Then, in addition to a cash award, the student's idea is put on tape with the student participating in the production. The PSA is then aired by the local stations. This means a lot to that student.

For students and others interested in the nature of the craft, we provide a series of programs and seminars in things like editing, sound production, video photography, studio lighting, etc. We also have drop-in luncheons with noted industry people and people who have impact on the industry.

And occasionally, we just have fun. We sponsor a screening of the national and international Clio Award winning commercials. A fall season premier party. A blooper bash. A night with the Bullets. A fundraiser at Chadwicks.

If you want to participate in the Academy or learn more about what we do, please give us a call.

John S. Douglass, President

THE NATIONAL ACADEMY OF TELEVISION ARTS AND SCIENCES
WASHINGTON, D.C. CHAPTER
9405 Russell Road
Silver Spring, MD 20910
(301) 587-3993

About BCDC

The Broadcasters' Child Development Center was an idea of the Washington Chapter of N.A.T.A.S. and several parents working in the Washington broadcast community in the late 70's. Through the initial support of N.A.T.A.S. and loans or gifts from WRC-TV, WTTG, WJLA-TV, WMAL radio and WDVM-TV, the Broadcasters' Child Development Center opened in 1980. It provides full time quality care for children ranging from 3 months to 5 years in age. Its infant program and the flexible contract hours were designed to meet the needs of those working in the broadcast industry. It serves the entire community, however, and is open to both broadcaster and non-broadcaster alike. Its emphasis on quality care and the growth and development of the child has made it a model for child care centers nationwide.

Index

APPETIZERS Antipasto, 10; Apple Canape, 11; Baked Brie, 12; Boursin Cheese, 13; Boursin Spread, 14; Chinese Meatballs, 15; Deviled Eggs, 14; Dragon's Breath, 19; Pickled Herring, 21; Horseradish Pie, 19; Shrimp Mousse, 23; Steak Tartare, 25.
APPLE Canapes, 11; Sauce, 136.
ARTICHOKE Soup, 26.

BANANA Bread, 202; Cake, 156; Pudding, 157.
BEANS Black beans and rice, 54; Black bean soup, 27; Feijoada, 93; Green beans, 142; Pasta and Bean Soup, 35.
BEEF Braised w/Polenta, 51; Brisket, 46; Burgundy, 47; Chinese Meatballs, 00; Choufleur, 48; Curry, 52; Flank steak with cheese, 94; Flank steak, marinated, 95; Meatloaf, 103; Pepper Steak, 106; Steak Tartare, 25; Swedish Meatballs, 126; w/Radishes, 49; Wellington, 50.
BEVERAGES Banana-Orange Frosted, 198; Bourbon Slush, 198; Eggnog, 199; Irish Tea, 200; Lime Punch, 201.
BREAD AND ROLLS Banana, 202; Bran muffins, 202; Brown, 205; Corn, 87; Popovers, lemon, 204; Popovers, parmesan, 204; Pumpkin, 203.
BROCCOLI Broccoli Bake, 136; Casserole, 56; Casserole w/chicken, 60.

CABBAGE Auntie's Salad, 38; Cabbage and Carrots, 137; w/pork, 112.
CAKE Banana Nut, 156; Brown Sugar Pound Cake, 189; Brownie Alaska, 161; Carrot, 163; Cheesecake, 164; Chocolate, 165; Double Diabolo, 170; Ice cream angel food, 176; Pound, 190; Refrigerator, 192; Sherry, 194.
CANDY English butter toffee, 194; Toffee bars, 196; Fudge, 173; Peanut butter fudge, 185.

CARROT w/cabbage, 137; Cake, 163; Soup, 30; Sweet & sour, 137.
CASSEROLE Broccoli, 56; Cauliflower, 139; Chicken Broccoli, 60; Chicken Divan, 64; Chicken, easy, 73; DoeDoe's, 92; Macaroni, 143; Potato, 149; Rice Pilaf, 149; Sweet Potato, 152; Tuna Noodle, 128; Zucchini & sausage, 134; Zucchini & tomato, 152.
CAULIFLOWER Beef Choufleur, 48; Casserole, 139.
CHEESE Baked brie, 12; Blue cheese w/flank steak, 94; Boursin cheese, 13; Boursin spread, 14; Broccoli bake, 136; Cheesecake, 164; Cheese and onion pie, 58; Cheese grits souffle, 57; Chicken-cheese rolls, 61; Chili cheese pie, 139; Cork's tripledecker, 55; Garden vegetables, 138; Grilled cheese sandwich, 97; Meatloaf, 103; Nachos, 20; Noodles parmesana, 142; Pita calzones, 108; Poor boy sandwich, 111.
CHICKEN Afro-dite barbequed, 70; Apricot salad, 39; Breasts w/cream, 72; Breasts w/sesame seeds, 59; Broccoli casserole, 60; Cheese roll, 61; Chinese, 71; Diet delight, 62; Divan, 64; Doro wat, 63; Easy casserole, 73; Emmies chicken, 74; Forty garlics, 65; Gloria, 66; Hawaiian, 75; Italian, 76; Juicy, 67; Lollipop, 77; Pelau, 67; Quickie gourmet, 78; Raspberry, 78; Sausage Skillet, 68; Schlemmerthop, 78; w/Shrimp, 69; Soup, 28; Southern fried, 80.
CHILI Chili, 81; Festival, 83; Frank's standard American, 84; w/Pinto beans, 82; Real, 86; Rescue squad, 85.
CHOCOLATE Blackbottom Miniatures, 158; Brownies, 160; Brownie Alaska, 161; Cake, moist, 165; Delights, 166; Double Diabolo cake, 170; English butter toffee, 194; English toffee cookies, 195; Fudge, 173; Fudge, microwave, 173; Fudgesauce, 174; Mousse, 167; Pie, 168; Pie, Mecklenburg, 184; Pie w/pecans, 169; Toffee bars, 196.

CLAMS Chowder, 30; Linguini w/sauce, 102.
COBBLER Fruit, 172.
COOKIES Black-bottom miniatures, 158; Brownies, 160; Brownies, Vinny's, 162; Chocolate delights, 166; Date sticks, 169; English Toffee, 195; Kipfel, 177; Lace crispies, 178; Lebkuchen, 179; Lemon bars, 180; Magic, 183; Rum balls, 193.
CRAB Cookin', 214; Dip, 17, 18; Crabcakes, 88, 89; Imperial, 90; Sauteed, 90; w/Shrimp, 91; Stuffed flounder, 96.
CRANBERRY Relish, 141.
CUCUMBER Salad, 39; Soup, 31.
CURRY Beef, 52; Indonesian dinner, 99.

DIP Crab, 17, 18; Dill, 16; Salmon, 20; Spinach, 24.
DRESSING Louisiana rice, 150.

EGGPLANT Bermuda breakfast, 53.
EGGS Bermuda breakfast, 53; Deviled, 14; French toast, 98; Green w/ham, 92; Ham & Egg Brunch, 98; Hearty omelettes, 103; Quiche, easy, 117; Quiche, 5 Minute, 116; w/salami & scallions, 119; Sausage ring, 120.

FISH (See also, CRAB, SHRIMP, TUNA); Flounder, stuffed, 96; Inlagd Sill (herring), 21; Salmon dip, 22; Shad roe, 121.
FRUIT (See also individual fruits); Cobbler, 172; Flan, 171.
FUDGE fudge, basic, 173; microwave, 173; peanut butter, 185; sauce, 174.

GRANOLA easy, 215.
GRAPES w/Grand Marnier, 175.

HAM Casserole, 56; w/Eggs Brunch, 98; w/Green eggs, 92.

TV Dinners
221

LASAGNA Never fail, 101; Seafood, 100.
LENTIL Soup, 34.

MISCELLANEOUS Boiling water, 208; Dinner Between 6 & 11, 211; Instant Italian, 216; Playdough, 217; Trash & Flash Dining, 212.
MOUSSE Chocolate, 167; Shrimp, 23.

OYSTERS Scalloped w/mushrooms, 105.

PASTA Green w/tomato sauce, 105; Lasagna, never fail, 100; Lasagna, seafood, 101; Linguini, bachelor, 207; Linguini, w/clam sauce, 102; Linguini, w/white conch, 133; Macaroni casserole, 143; Noodles, Buckaroo, 145; Noodles, parmesana, 142; Piquant Veal, 129; Skinny spaghetti salad, 124; Spaghetti Carbonara, 122; Tortellini, 127; Tri-color salad, 43.
PEACH Sweet peach delight, 186.
PEPPERS Red with snow peas, 153; Shrimp w/green pepper, 124; Stuffed, 107.
PIE AND PIE CRUST Cheese & Onion, 58; Chocolate, Lea's, 168; Chocolate Pecan, 169; Crazy Crust, 118; JC's "Fruit", 171; Key Lime, 182; Lemon Meringue, 181; Mecklenburg, 184; Pecan, 187; Sweet Potato, 189.
PINEAPPLE Pineapple Bake, 188.
PIZZA L'il Pizza, 207; Pizza, basic, 109; Yia Yia's, 110.
POPCORN Harvest, 215.
PORK Charles, 112; Chinese meatballs, 15; Chops w/sour cream, 113; Indonesian kabobs, 114; Roast, 115.
POTATO Casserole, hash brown, 149; Casserole, sweet potato, 152; French fries, 147; New w/cumin vinaigrette, 148; Pie, Sweet potato, 189; Salad, German, 146.
PUDDING Banana, 157; Irish Coffee, 177.
PUMPKIN Bread, 203.

QUICHE Easy, 117; 5 Minute, 116.

RADISH w/beef stirfry, 49.
RASPBERRY Chicken, 78; Tart, 191.
RELISH Cranberry, 141.
RICE w/black beans, 54; Casserole, 149; Chili cheese pie, 139; Dressing, 151; London poverty mush, 208.

SALAD Auntie's, 38; Chicken-Apricot, 39; Cucumber w/yogurt, 39; German Potato, 146; Frosty strawberry, 40; Pasta, 43; Layered Lettuce, 41; w/Pepper Steak, 106; Sesame seed, 42; Skinny Spaghetti, 124; Spinach w/strawberry, 40; Tuna, 44.
SALAD DRESSING All purpose, 36; Celery seed, 37; Leon's secret, 38.
SANDWICH Grilled cheese, 97; Pita Calzone, 108; Poor boy, 111; Tripledecker, 55.
SAUCE Dan-Dan w/noodles, 132; Fudge, 174; Marinara, 127; Spaghetti, 123; White Conch, 133.
SAUSAGE w/chicken, 68; Ring, 120; w/Zucchini, 134.
SHRIMP w/Chicken, 69; Crab bake, 91; w/green peppers, 124; Seafood Lasagna, 101; Nelson, 125.
SOUFFLE Cheese grits, 57.
SOUP Artichoke, 26; Black bean, 27; Clam chowder, 30; Carrot, 30; Chicken, 28; Cucumber, 31; Gazpacho, 30; Lentil, 34; Pasta & Bean, 35.
SPINACH Dip, hot, 23; Dip, in loaf, 24; Dragon's Breath, 19; Salad w/strawberry, 40.
SQUASH Butternut w/anise, 148.
STRAWBERRY Salad, frosty, 40; Salad, w/spinach, 40.

TUNA Casserole, 128; Salad, 44.

VEAL Kidneys, 130; Piquant, 129; Tonnato, 131.

VEGETABLES (See also specific vegetables); Cheesy garden, 138; Cold marin 140; w/dill dip, 16; Mesquite fever, 1 Ratatouille, 151; Snow peas and pepp 153.

ZUCCHINI Tomato casserole, 152; w/Sausage, 134.

TV Dinners

Contributors

Adams, Rich, 116, 85
Aiken, Ann, 19
Alexander, Dan, 205
Altman, Susan, 186
Antosh, Renee, 139, 108, 69, 204
Atkins, Kate, 152
Bain, Jackson, 114
Barnes, Gordon, 53
Beatrice, Ken, 183
Bell, Lageris, 70
Bell, Steve, 160
Berry, Paul, 165
Blunt, Kathy, 199
Bostic, Jeff, 29
Bowers, Jeanne, 90
Brown, Vinny, 162
Bruno, Hal, 119
Buchanan, Mike, 145
Burch, Vivian, 78
Butler, Sandra, 90
Bye, Kathy, 23, 40, 120, 30
Campbell, Arch, 86
Campbell, Karen, 91
Campbell, Stephanie, 184
Cerri, Bill, 19
Chapman, Robin, 163
Clarke, Jim, 50
Corcoran, John, 55
Cosmos, Bill, 110
Davenport, Faye, 172
Dawson, Mimi Weyforth, 37
Desantis, Mark, 123
Douglass, John, 105, 134, 167, 215
Drummond, Tammy, 164
Dukehart, Tad, 95
Duke, Paul, 121
Dyszel, Dick, 61
Elliott, Jim, 73
Ellis, Patrick, 67
Ely-Epstein, Diana, 12
Fang, Linda, 15
Farber, Gail, 105
Fava, Gloria, 66, 131
Fertig-Dykes, Susan, 99
Fine, Holly, 24
Fine, Paul, 215
Fitzgerald, Gena, 216, 14, 35
Flannigan, Gail, 144, 27
Foxx, Dave, 67
Gales, Jaquiline, 28
Gaskins, Yolanda, 161
Gauser, Tom, 182
Gibson, Valeria, 201
Goldsmith, John, 212
Gordon, Gerald, 177
Gorham, Joe, 103
Grant, Felix, 93
Grunbaum, Barbara, 139, 33
Guttenberg, Stan, 194
Habteab, Jean, 63
Hagedorn, Steve, 202
Harden, Frank, 21
Harnden, Glenn, 54

Harris, Glenn, 137
Hart, Betsy, 72
Hart, Joe, 98
Hayward, J.C., 171
Helsley, Bob, 102
Henderson, Karen, 140
Herzog, Frank, 84
Hoiland, Harold, 177, 178
Holliday, Johnny, 11
Hollingsworth, Jim, 185
Hubert, Judy, 80
Hunter, Jack, 103
Jackson, Dimetrius, 147
Jackson, Donna, 111
Jarriel, Tom, 60
Jones, Morris, 82
Kanner, Bob, 158
Kavenaugh, Chuck, 173
Kingsley, Ellen, 36
King, Susan, 211, 74
Klug, Scott and Tess, 42
Knight, Fred, 188
Knight, Susan, 17
Korzec, Heidi, 136
Kumaki, Marge, 156, 77
Kurtis, Bill, 191
Lacore, Madeline, 38
Laine, Susan, 34
Lalos, Mary, 18
Laurent, Lawrence, 128
Lawson, Pat, 143
Lechner, Susan, 23
Lee, Lorraine, 112
Lehrer, Jim, 20
Lerner, Myla, 198
Levey, Bob, 153
Levine, Irving R., 32
Lewis, Dan, 48
Lewis, Mike, 59, 148
Lively, Peyton, 101
Loy, Joel, 169, 51
Lyon, John, 83
Marchesand, Carole, 49
Martin, Samara, 58
Matthews, Kathleen, 175
Mayhugh, Bill, 97
McBride, Bob, 200
McCracken, Jan Brown, 180, 40, 138
McMillon, Doris, 127
Mesard, Sharman, 64
Mesirow, Tod, 208
Mielke, Ginger, 56
Minter, Isaac, 173
Mixon, Karolyn, 79
Morton, Bruce, 109
Mullally, Terry, 118, 117
Mullen, Corrin, 172, 124
Murphy, Fran, 151
Murphy, John, 39
Murphy, Gary, 81
Nelson, Kathy Filosi, 194
Nelson, Larry, 125
Nesbitt, Frank, 122

Nuell, David, 16
Ockershausen, Andy, 170
Orphan, Georgia, 52
O'Brien, Tim, 26
Pastoor, Sandy, 137
Peterson, Gordon, 71
Pollak, Ruth, 174
Povich, Maury, 181
Powell, Carol, 195
Pumphrey, Diana Clark, 75
Rabin, Stephen, 10
Randolph, Carol, 41
Reece, Paul, 129
Rehm, Diane, 130
Rice, Joseph, 106
Ritter, R. Randolph, 94, 133
Roane, Andrea, 107
Robinson, Angela, 80
Rosenberg, Min, 166
Rudolph, Cynthia, 124
Sarginson, Wes, 126
Sawyer, Forrest, 115
Scott, Willard, 189, 57
Seeger, Frances Stachow, 100
Seeger, Mark, 44
Shainman, Larry, 210
Shippy-Koebbe, Marlene, 38, 92, 157
Shriver, Maria, 89
Silimeo, Debra, 78
Simon, Pam, 149, 22
Smilovitz, Bernie, 209
Smith, Jack, 65
Smith, Paul, 92
Southerland, Sandra, 76
Staake, Sue Ann, 179, 169
Stamberg, Susan, 141
Starling, Walt, 17
Steadman, Arthur, 207
Sullivan, Kathleen, 192
Takanishi, Ruby, 202
Talley, Deb, 62
Tenenbaum, Henry, 25
Terry, Janet, 189
Thompson, Jan, 198, 43
Thompson, Lea, 168
Thomson, Dave, 47, 98
Todd, Saralee, 46
Trueblood, Toni, 176
Trumbull, Bill, 113
Turney, Ed, 214
Uncle Johnny, 207
Weaver, Jackson, 88
Weaver, Sandy, 187
Weiss, Fred, 146
Werner, Lauren, 204, 31, 142, 152
Williams, Andrea, 193
Wilson, Stephanie B., 203
Winn-Ritzenberg, Katy, 132, 39, 142
Wnek, Madilee, 190
Wolff, Perry, 136
Woodside, Scott, 196

Order Form

Please send me _____ copies of *"TV Dinners ... And Other Media Munchies"* at $7.95 each. (Add $2.00 for postage and handling.)

Enclosed is my check or money order for _____
(Make checks payable to N.A.T.A.S. "TV Dinners")

Send To:

Name _____
Street _____
City _____
State _____ Zip _____

Send your order to:
   National Academy of Television Arts and Sciences
   Washington Chapter
   9405 Russell Road
   Silver Spring, Maryland 20910